THE KETO CROCK POT COOKBOOK

Top 60 Easy Keto Crock Pot Recipes for Rapid Fat Loss

By William Cook

TABLE OF CONTENTS

INTRODUCTION

You might have heard of a Keto diet plan, but may not have an exact idea about what it exactly is or you might be hearing it for the very first time.

Whatever category you fall into, don't worry, I'm here to help you. As you landed up here, it means that you have some serious interest in knowing about diet and would like to get a handy list of easy Keto Crock Pot recipes for fat loss. It's quite evident that the well-known advice to "Eat less and exercise more" for weight loss is not working for all of us. It is a fact that a significant portion of dieters who lose weight, gain it back quickly. So the real question is, is there an ultimate solution to this universal problem? As per my experience and research in this area, I have come up to a conclusion that Keto diet is something which can help solve this problem of weight loss.

Ketosis is significant for your weight loss as it helps suppress your appetite unlike other diets and it also provides mental clarity and increases focus. Moreover, for preparing Keto meals, crock pots are using, which will increase the nutritional benefits like anything. Once you get on track with Keto diet, you will no longer have to worry about your appetite. No more counting calories and no more crazy spot exercises to reduce your belly.

If this idea seems appealing to you, continue reading and get ready to be on a Keto diet with delicious and healthy crock pot prepared meal plans. However, if you still have some questions, we will cover all of the details in the upcoming chapter so that you can get started.

WHAT IS A KETO DIET?

Keto diet is the short form of ketogenic diet, which is a low-carbohydrate diet that puts your body in a fat burning state. In this diet, your body will produce ketones which are converted into energy later on.

The Keto diet is gaining popularity like anything, and it is a dietician's nightmare as well. Everybody these days is raving about Keto diet, and you might be hearing about it so much. In this chapter let's get into the details of why people are talking about this all the time.

How does Keto diet work?

The special diet forces human body to burn fats instead of carbohydrates. Now, the carbohydrates in food get converted to glucose which is transported all around bloodstream and is utilized to fuel brain functioning. However, as there is a very little carbohydrate in the diet, your liver will convert it to fatty acids and ketone bodies. These ketones will pass into your brain, and it replaces glucose and function as an energy source. Ketones are nothing but three water-soluble molecules namely, Beta-hydroxybutyrate, Acetoacetate and a breakdown product of these 2, Acetone. Ketones are created by the human liver when glucose is not available as an energy source.

BENEFITS OF THE KETOGENIC DIET

Kills your appetite

Hunger is a killer that destroys everything when it comes to a diet plan. The best things about Keto diet are they kill your hunger pangs or appetite. When you eat fewer carbs and increase the protein intake, you eventually end up eating fewer calories.

Reduces abdomen fat

Depending on where your body fat has stored, it affects your health both positively and in an adverse manner. Having fat stored as visceral which stored in the abdominal cavity can lead to metabolic dysfunction. Keto diet is very efficient when it comes to burning belly fat due to its low-carb nature.

Decreases triglycerides

Triglycerides are fat molecules associated with heart disease risk. Carbohydrate intake is the main reason for your triglycerides to elevate up. When you are on a low carbohydrate diet, it tends to reduce the triglyceride level in your blood effectively.

Increases good cholesterol

Good cholesterol or high-density lipoproteins (HDL) are lipoproteins that carry cholesterol around the bloodstream. HDL takes cholesterol away from your body and to the liver so that it can reuse again. Consuming fat is the best way to increase HDL in your blood, and when you are on a Keto diet, your good cholesterol level rises.

WHAT IS A CROCK POT?

A common doubt regarding crock pot is whether a crock pot and slow cooker are same or not. Like many people, earlier, I also assumed that both were the same. However, it turns out that both aren't same, although crock pot is a type of slow cooker. There are a lot of similarities between a crock pot and slow cooker, and while the crock pot is a slow cooker, not all slow cookers are crock pots. Hope you have got my point clearly now.

Let's quickly get into some history of crock pots. The crock pot hit the market as a bean cooker in the late 1970s. Later the brand expanded its repertoire and included various types of dishes. Afterwards, the company redesigned the cook pot and added handles and a glass lid to it, and the cooker christened as 'Crock Pot'. As per the popular belief, a person named Irving Naxon got the patent for this bean cooker which he named as 'Naxon Beanery'. He sold the design to rival manufacturing which again rebranded the beanery and displayed it in the market as a 'Crock Pot'.

Now, the term crock pot itself has become a general term that is used to refer types of slow cookers, but with the real crock pot, the crock is a container with heating elements on the bottom and in the sides of it.

Crock pots are economical and specially designed to cook budget-friendly ingredients to prepare a healthy meal for the whole family. The least amount of effort required is the top highlight of cooking using a crock pot. Cooking in a low heat brings out the savory of flavors and gives the meals an extra zest. Another great attribute of the crock pot is the incredible flavoring it produces. The food cooked using the mixed juices of the ingredients bring in the deep and rich flavor that other cooking methods are not able to achieve.

When you are buying a crock pot, the size and shape need to give proper consideration. Oval crock pots will help you to cook larger meals whereas small, and round crock pots help you to prepare for a small family.

HOW DOES A CROCK POT WORK?

From a technical perspective, a crock pot is a kind of electrical heating oven that features either porcelain or ceramic pot fitting correctly into the crock and comes with a glass lid to secure the moisture inside.

The crock pot comes in mainly two heat settings, high and low. The low temperature is around 70°C, and the highest is 150°C, but there are some models which also come with a warm setting. It is mainly using to cook tough cuts of meat or dishes that require slow cooking. The direct heat from the pot, long cooking hour, continued steaming in a tight container will destroy any bacteria that is in the meat. The crock pot simmers the food at a low temperature, and hence it is a type of safe cooking process.

The crock pots start cooking at a low heat and later the temperature increases to a higher degree over a matter of hours. During cooking, you don't have to add a lot of water as it follows a very slow mode of cooking. However, when it comes to cooking meat, it is recommended to add adequate water as it helps in keeping the meat at a particular temperature. Some crock pot models automatically set themselves to 70 degrees Celsius and keep all the liquid from evaporating, and finally, you will get dried perfectly cooked meat. Advanced crock pots allow you to program when the temperature changes have to take place.

THE DIFFERENCE BETWEEN A CROCK POT AND SLOW COOKER

It's a common practice for people to use the term slow cooker and crock pot interchangeable, but it doesn't mean that both are same. As said earlier, not all slow cookers are crock pot and crock pot is just a type of slow cooker. Both have its similarities and differences that make them two different things in some aspects. Now that you know in details about crock pot and how it functions, let's look into the slow cooker and its functioning. As crock pot is a type of slow cooker, every slow cooker consists same components as that of a crock pot. Slow cookers come with a pot, heating element surrounding its body and a glass lid. The significant difference of slow cookers in general when compared to crock pots is that instead of porcelain or ceramic pot, a slow cooker features a metal pot.

Unlike crock pots, the container or the metal crock sits on the base where the heating element is present. The hot plate under the crock will have more heat settings than a crock pot as well. The slow cooker will contain a heating setting ranging from 1 to 5 with 1 being the low-temperature setting and 5 being the highest setting.

Slow cookers and crock pots come in different sizes to suit the specific purpose of a family. The slow cooker is much lighter than crock pots as they don't have metal pot. As crock pots are of stoneware, you also supposed to handle it with care to avoid breaking of the bowl. Both the crock pot and slow cookers are ideal for cooking soups, vegetables, and meat.

REASONS WHY YOU NEED A CROCK POT FOR YOUR KETO DIET

The toughest part of being on a food diet is sticking to it. No matter how attractive or versatile the menu, you get to feel bored after sometime. Moreover, when you are on a diet, meal preparation can be a daunting task as your family don't need necessarily follow the same menu. So the meal prep part also has to be easy when it comes to starting a diet. For a Keto diet, the best way is to prepare your meals in a crock pot.

There are many reasons. The easy meal preparation and less cooking time are the significant advantages of using a crock pot. Let's check the benefits in details.

Cooks less expensive cuts of meat

Expensive cuts of meat are more comfortable to cook in your oven or traditional stove. However, when you are on a Keto diet, you will feel good when you can save money in specific areas. If you cook meals in a crock pot, it can also prepare less expensive cuts of meat properly. When you use the regular stove to cook such types of meat cuts, the meat will not get tender within a short time. However, when it comes to cooking in a crock pot, slow cooking yields adequately prepared and yummy food.

Meals contain less fat

When you cook in the crock pot, as the food cooks in its own juice and essence, you don't have to add any extra oil or butter to cook the food quickly. Hence, the final meal contains less fat when compared to other cooking techniques.

Retains nutrition

Again, due to the facts that the food gets cooked in the juice of the ingredients, it retains more vitamins and other nutrients when compared to the food that prepared in conventional style cooking. As it cooked for long hours at low temperature with the lids closed, all nutrients will remain in the meal.

WHY YOU NEED THESE RECIPES

Try searching for Keto recipes and you will get lots and lots of recipes on your computer screen. I know how tough it is to browse through the giant unsorted list of recipes. Sadly, most of the recipes come with undesirable ingredients that might not be suitable for all. To save your time and to make things easier for you, I have come up with these 60 easy and convenient crock pot recipes that aid your weight loss efforts.

These crock pot recipes improve the odds and urge you to eat healthy home-cooked food every day without any hassle. When you are ready with deliciously prepared home food, you will be less tempted to eat outside. Crock pot recipes are super healthy options as they cooked in the broth without the need for oil. You can combine vegetables and lean proteins all in one pot so that your meals boast nutrients from various essential food groups. Cooking your own Keto meal will help you control the salt, sugar, fat, carbs, protein and calories that go into your meal.

Also, the recipes come with the ingredient measurements, and nutritional facts mentioned clearly so that you don't have to worry thinking about the values.

KETO CROCK POT BREAKFAST

1. CROCK POT MEXICAN BREAKFAST CASSEROLE

Preparation time: 15 minutes | **Cooking time:** 2 hours and 30 minutes | **Servings:** 10

INGREDIENTS:

- Pork Sausage Roll - 12 ounces (I prefer Jones Dairy)
- Garlic powder - ½ teaspoon
- Coriander – ½ teaspoon
- Cumin - 1 teaspoon
- Salsa – 1 cup
- Chili fine powder - 1 teaspoon
- Salt - ¼ teaspoon
- Pepper - ¼ teaspoon
- Eggs - 10
- Milk low fat - 1 cup
- Cheese (Pepper Jack if available) - 1 cup
- Toppings if required: Avocado salsa, sour cream, cilantro – as per preference

COOKING METHOD:

1. Put a pan on low flame and cook pork sausage until it leaves its pink color.
2. Add all the spices given and let it cool and set for some time.
3. Now take a medium bowl and whisk eggs and milk together.
4. Add the pork to the eggs and stir well so that they get mixed properly.
5. Take a crock pot and grease its bottom and pour the mixture you prepared.
6. Cook on high flame for 2 hours and 30 minutes.
7. You can put seasonal toppings on it according to your taste.

Tips for fast cooking: Once the pork sausage heated thoroughly, cover it with an aluminum foil about 45 minutes, which will make it much tender and save further cooking time.

NUTRITIONAL VALUES

Fat: 24g | Cholesterol: 231g | Sodium: 749mg | Carbohydrates: 5.2g | Protein: 17.9g | Dietary Fiber: 2.6g | Potassium: 454mg

2. CAULIFLOWER HASH BROWNS BREAKFAST CASSEROLE

Preparation time: 15 minutes | **Cooking time**: 5-7 hours | **Serving**: 10

INGREDIENTS

- Eggs - 12
- Milk - ½ cup
- Dry mustard - ½ teaspoon
- Kosher salt - 1 teaspoon
- Pepper - ½ teaspoon
- Cauliflower, shredded - 1 head
- Additional salt and pepper to season the layers – as required
- Small onion, diced - 1
- Packaged pre-cooked breakfast sausages, sliced – 5 ounces
- Shredded cheddar cheese – 8 ounces

METHOD

1. First of all, grease a 6-quart slow cooker properly with cooking spray.
2. Mix well all the item likes the eggs, milk, dry mustard, salt, and pepper.
3. From the shredded cauliflower, take one-third portion and layer it in the bottom of the crock pot. After that place one-third of the sliced onion on top.
4. Use pepper and salt to season and top it with one-third portion of sausage and cheese.
5. Repeat the same process by maintaining two layers.
6. Pour the eggs mixture over slow cooker
7. Cook on low for 5-7 hours and wait until eggs set properly and the top color is browned.

Easy cooking tips: You can also cook the recipe by using instant pot cooker, which can reduce the cooking time considerably. Check the instruction of instant pot cooker, before using.

NUTRITIONAL VALUES

Calories: 87.7 | Total Fat: 5.4g | Cholesterol: 1mg | Total Carbohydrates: 2.2g | Dietary Fiber: 1.2g | Protein: 8g

3. CROCK POT BREAKFAST CASSEROLE

Preparation time: 15-20 minutes | **Cooking time**: 6 hours | **Servings**: 8

INGREDIENTS

- Brown jicama, hashed or brown daikon radish - 4 cups
- Cooked, crumbled, and drained bacon slices - 12 ounces
- Cooked, drained and grounded sausage - 1 pound
- Onion, sweet yellow, chopped - 1
- Diced green bell pepper – 1
- Fresh mushroom, sliced - 1 to ½ cups
- Fresh spinach - 1 to ½ cups
- Shredded cheese - 2 cups (Monterrey Jack preferred)
- Feta cheese, shredded - ½ cup
- Eggs - 1 dozen
- Heavy white cream - 1 cup

- Salt - 1 tablespoon
- Pepper - 1 tablespoon

METHOD

1. First of all, put a layer of hashed browns in the bottom of the cooker with low flame.
2. Then put the layer of bacon and sausage over it.
3. Put all the spices upon the layer.
4. Now take a bowl and whisk the eggs, cream, salt and pepper together.
5. Pour the mixture of eggs in the cooker.
6. Cover it and let it cook for 6 hours on high flame or for 12 hours on low flame.

Fast cooking tips: Using an instant pot cooker can reduce the cooking time considerably. Also, always use pre-cooked ingredients, which can also reduce the cooking time.

NUTRITIONAL VALUES

Calories: 443 | Carbohydrates: 8g | Fat: 38g | Fiber: 2g | Protein: 18g

4. KETO SLOW COOKER BACON-MUSHROOM BREAKFAST

Preparation time: 15 minutes | **Cooking time**: 1 hours 45 minutes | **Servings:** 4

INGREDIENTS

- Bacon large, sliced – 3½ Ounces
- White mushrooms, chopped – 2½ Ounces
- Eggs – 6 Nos.
- Shallots, chopped – 3 Tablespoons
- Bell pepper, chopped - ¾ Cup
- Kale leaves large, shredded – 8 Nos.
- Ghee – 1 Tablespoons.
- Parmesan cheese – 1 Cup
- Avocado and green leaves (Optional)

INSTRUCTIONS:

1. Clean the kale leaves, remove the hard stems and chop into small pieces.
2. In a skillet cook the bacon, till it becomes crispy and add mushrooms, red pepper, and shallot.
3. Add kale and cut down the flame and let the kale become tender in the skillet.
4. Now take a medium bowl and beat all eggs, add pepper and salt.
5. In the crock pot, add ghee and let it become hot. Spread the ghee on all side of the cooker.
6. Put the sautéed vegetable into the base of the cooker.
7. Spread the cheese over the vegetables.
8. Then, add the beaten eggs on top.
9. Just stir it gently.
10. Set the cooker on low heat and cook for about 6 hours.
11. Serve hot with sliced avocado and green leaves.

Tips: Instead of ghee, you can also use half ounce of butter. Similarly, it is not necessary to use parmesan cheese; you may use any suitable cheese. Also, limit the quantity of red pepper as per your choice. Read the cooking recommendation of your cooker manual to make sure that your cooker can give the required warmness for 6 hours, and never spoil your dish.

NUTRITIONAL VALUES:

Calories: 313 | Carb: 4g | Protein: 22.9g | Fat: 22.2g | Potassium: 503mg | Magnesium: 65mg

5. KETO SAUSAGE & EGG CASSEROLE

Preparation time: 15-20 minutes | **Cooking time**: 4-5 hours | **Servings**: 6-8

INGREDIENTS

- Large Eggs - 12
- Pork sausage links, cooked and sliced – 12 ounces
- Broccoli, finely chopped – 1
- Cheddar Shredded – 1 cup
- Whipping cream - ¾ cup
- Garlic cloves, minced - 2
- Salt – to taste (½ teaspoon)
- Pepper – ½ tablespoon

METHOD

1. Take a 6quart ceramic slow cooker and grease its interior.
2. Put one layer of broccoli, half portion of the cheese and half part of sausage into the ceramic cooker. Repeat the layering and put all the ingredients in the cooker.
3. Take a large bowl, and mix eggs, garlic, whipping cream, pepper and salt thoroughly.
4. Transfer the mix over the layered ingredients in the ceramic cooker.
5. Cover and cooker for about 5 hours.
6. Make sure the edges are not overcooked.
7. Check the center and make sure your finger bounce back when touching.

Cooking tip: If you want to cook on high heat, just cook it for 2-3 hours. But do it carefully.

NUTRITIONAL VALUES

Calories: 484 | Fat: 38.86g | Cholesterol: 399mg | Potassium: 8mg | Carbohydrates: 5.39g | Dietary Fiber: 1.18g | Sodium: 858mg | Protein: 26.13g

6. SLOW COOKER BREAKFAST FRITTATA

Preparation time: 10 minutes | **Cooking time**: 2-3 hours | **Servings**: 6

INGREDIENTS

- Eggs – 8
- Cooked sausage - 1½ cups
- Spinach, frozen, drained - ¾ cup
- Black pepper – ½ teaspoon
- Chopped onion – ½ cup
- Salt to taste
- Red bell pepper - 1½ cups

Freezer container

- Freezer bag – 1 gallon size

METHOD

1. Take a slow cooker and grease its bottom.
2. Mix the frozen spinach, red onion, black pepper, eggs, sausage, and red pepper in the slow cooker.
3. Cook for about 2-3 hours until the frittata set firm.
4. You can also serve it.

Freeze it for later use: You can keep it for later use by keeping it in the freezer container and microwave it for 30-60 seconds before use.

NUTRITIONAL VALUES

Calories: 238 | Fat: 16g | Cholesterol: 98 mg | Sodium: 844mg | Potassium: 75mg | Carbohydrate: 3g | Protein: 20g

7. KETO SLOW COOKER EGG & MUSHROOM BREAKFAST

Preparation time: 15 minutes | **Cooking time**: 6 hours | **Servings**: 4

INGREDIENTS

- Mushrooms, chopped - 1 cup
- Bacon large - 3
- Eggs - 6
- Chopped shallots - 3 tablespoons
- Bell pepper, red - ½ cup
- Shredded, kale leaves - 8 large
- Parmesan cheese, shredded - 1 cup
- Butter or ghee - 1 tablespoon
- Pepper - ¼ spoon
- Salt to taste
- Spinach - for dressing

- Avocado, sliced - for dressing
- Virgin olive oil - for dressing

METHOD

1. Wash, clean and slice the bacon
2. Wash, clean and remove the stem of the kale and chop it nicely.
3. Take a pan and cook bacon until it becomes crispy.
4. Add mushroom, pepper, and shallot and continue heating until it becomes soft.
5. Now add kale and switch off the stove and let the kale wilt.
6. Take a small mixing bowl and beat the eggs, with pepper and salt.
7. Put on the slow cooker and add some butter.
8. Grease the inside of the cooker properly with the butter.
9. Transfer the sautéed vegetables to the cooker.
10. Spread the cheese over it.
11. Add the beaten egg on top of the mixture.
12. Stir well and slow heat about 6 hours.
13. You may occasionally check the food after 4 hours.
14. Check with your finger to bounce back.
15. Serve it with sliced avocado, spread with spinach dressed in olive oil.

Cooking tips: Try using fresh vegetables and mushrooms, which shall have nutritional values. Similarly, if you don't like slow cooking, you can cook the crock breakfast in fast cooking which can reduce cooking time to less than half.

NUTRITIONAL VALUES

Total Carbs: 6.1g | Fiber: 2.1g | Net Carbs: 4g | Fat: 22.2g | Protein: 22.9g | Energy: 313kcal | Magnesium: 65mg | Potassium: 503mg

8. EGG, SPINACH, AND HAM BREAKFAST CASSEROLE

Preparation time: 10 minutes | **Cooking time**: 1 hours and 30 minutes | **Servings**: 6

INGREDIENTS

- Large eggs - 6
- Salt - ½ teaspoon
- Black pepper - ¼ teaspoon
- Milk - ¼ cup
- Greek yogurt - ½ cup
- Thyme - ½ teaspoon
- Onion powder - ½ teaspoon
- Garlic powder - ½ teaspoon
- Diced mushrooms - ⅓ cup
- Baby spinach (packed) – 1 cup
- Shredded pepper jack cheese – 1 cup
- Ham, diced – 1 cup

METHOD

1. Mix eggs, salt, pepper, milk, yogurt, thyme, onion powder, garlic powder properly in a bowl.
2. Add mushrooms, spinach, cheese, ham, and stir.
3. Now take a 6-quart slow cooker and spray with non-stick cooking spray.
4. Pour eggs mixture into the cooker and put on slow.
5. Cover and cook on high for 90-120 minutes until eggs appropriately set.
6. Slice and serve for breakfast or dinner.

Fast cooking tips: Use pre-cooked mushrooms to reduce cooking time.

NUTRITIONAL VALUES

Calories: 155.6 | Total Fat: 8.7g | Cholesterol: 86.1mg | Sodium: 758.8mg | Total Carbs: 2.5g | Dietary Fiber: 0.3g | Protein: 15.6g

9. KETO CROCK POT PIE

Preparation time: 10 minutes | **Cooking time:** 8 hours | **Servings:** 6

INGREDIENTS

- Pork sausages, chopped - 2 cups
- Eggs, well beaten - 8
- Dried basil - 2 teaspoon
- Dried thyme - 2 teaspoon
- Chopped squash - 2 cups
- Coconut oil - 2 tablespoon
- Onion, finely chopped - 1
- Pumpkin, finely sliced - 1½ cups
- Garlic powder - 1 teaspoon
- Paprika powder - 1 teaspoon
- Pepper - as required
- Salt - to taste

METHOD

1. Take a crock pot and pour coconut oil and set aside
2. Put all the ingredients in large mixing bowl and mix thoroughly
3. Keep it aside for slow cooking in the night.
4. Your pie will be ready by morning.
5. Just warm it and serve.

Cooking tip: If you can use, precooked sausages, that can reduce the cooking time considerably. Similarly, if you don't like the taste of coconut oil, you can use ghee.

NUTRITIONAL VALUES

Fat: 32g | Carbohydrates: 7g | Fiber: 3g | Protein: 20g

10. CROCK POT SAUSAGE & EGG BREAKFAST

Preparation time: 15 minutes | **Cooking time**: 5 hours | **Servings**: 8

INGREDIENTS

- Broccoli, chopped – 1 Medium size
- Sausage, cooked & sliced – 12 Ounces
- Eggs – 5
- Whipped cream - ¾ Cup
- Cheddar shredded – 1 Cup
- Clove garlic, minced – 2 Nos.
- Salt - ½ Teaspoon
- Pepper to taste

DIRECTION:

1. Grease a 6-quart crockpot.
2. Place broccoli in one layer, half portion of the sausage and cheese into the crockpot.
3. Repeat layering the remaining portion.
4. Whisk eggs with whipping cream, pepper, salt, and garlic until appropriately combined.
5. Transfer the mix on top the layered ingredients in the crockpot.
6. Cover the lid and set to cook for about 5 hours.
7. Check occasionally to see if the edges become brown and center is set.
8. Serve hot or cold.

Tips: You can try with any sausages available in the store. Also, you can try experimenting with fresh vegetables. If you like spicy dish, you can add hot/green chili as per your preference.

NUTRITIONAL VALUE

Cal: 484 | Carb: 5.39g | Fat: 38.86g | Protein: 26.13g | Dietary Fiber: 1.18g | Sodium: 858mg

11. KETO SOUP WITH MISO

Preparation time: 15 minutes | **Cooking time:** 8 hours | **Serving:** 4

INGREDIENTS:

- Chopped onion - 1 medium
- Miso, white good quality - 2 tablespoon
- Olive oil - 4 tablespoons
- Garlic, minced - 1 teaspoon
- Broccoli flowerets - 1 cup
- Zucchini, chopped - 1 cup
- Celery stalks, cut into pieces - 2 stalks
- Pumpkin, diced - 1 cup
- Pepper as required
- Salt to taste

METHOD:

1. Take a crock pot and put 2 tablespoons olive oil and keep aside.
2. Then take a large skillet, put 2 tablespoons of oil and heat it.
3. Add onion, garlic, pumpkin, celery to the heating skillet by sprinkling bit of salt.
4. Sauté for 5 minutes
5. Transfer this mixture to the crock pot and put all other ingredients.
6. Now pour about 4 cups of water and salt to taste.
7. Stir well.
8. Take 3 tablespoons of water and mix the Miso and add to the crock pot.
9. Put it in the slow cooker for about 8 hours.
10. Serve warm

Cooking Tip: Since it is a slow cooking method, it is better to set the cooking during your bedtime. So that by morning your breakfast will be ready.

NUTRITION FACTS

Carbohydrate: 6g | Net Carbs: 4.86g | Fat: 19g | Fiber: 3g | Protein: 12g

12. LOW CARB BANANA BREAD BREAKFAST

Preparation: 5 minutes | **Cooking time:** 2 Hour 30 minutes | **Serve:** 16 slices

INGREDIENTS:

- Banana, mashed – 1 Medium size
- Butter, melted - ½ Cup
- Coconut oil – 3 Tablespoons
- Eggs – 6 Nos.
- Coconut flour - ⅓ Cup
- Xanthan gum - ½ Cup
- Almond flour - ⅔ Cup
- Vanilla extract – 1 Teaspoon
- Low carb sweetener - ½ Cup
- Stevia powder, concentrated - ¼ Teaspoon
- Baking powder – 1 Teaspoon
- Walnuts, chopped - ½ Cup
- Salt to taste

DIRECTIONS:

1. In a medium bowl mix all the dry ingredients, such as coconut flour, baking powder, almond flour, erythritol sweetener and xanthan gum.
2. Keep it aside.
3. Now in the processor add coconut oil, vanilla extract, eggs, mashed banana, butter and mix it slowly.
4. Continue process until combined well.
5. Add the dry ingredients and continue the batter gain a uniform consistency.
6. Sprinkle chopped walnuts into the batter.
7. Transfer the batter to the slow crockpot cooker.
8. Line the crockpot with aluminum foil before you transfer the batter.
9. Cover the crockpot with a paper towel over the edges and close the lid.
10. In doing, the paper towel can absorb the moisture released during cooking.
11. Set the cooker for two and half hours.
12. Check the dish after two hours and make sure the top portion becomes brown.
13. Insert a toothpick and check out if it comes out dry.
14. Once done, remove it to serving plate.
15. Serve after the dish settled down.

Tips: You can reduce the egg to 3 and add ¼ cup low carb milk.

NUTRITIONAL VALUE

Cal: 193 | Carb: 6g | Fat: 18g | Cholesterol: 85mg | Potassium: 71mg | Sodium: 168mg | Protein: 4g

KETO CROCK POT
APPETIZERS & SNACKS

1. DELICIOUS BOURBON AND GLAZED COCKTAIL SAUSAGES

Preparation time: 10 minutes | **Cooking time:** 4 hours | **Servings:** 12

INGREDIENTS

- Cooked and smoked Polish sausage or turkey sausage - 16, sliced into 1-inch size.
- Apricot syrup, low-sugar type -⅓ cup
- Pure maple syrup - 3 tablespoons
- Crushed quick-cooking tapioca - 1 teaspoons
- Bourbon or water - 1 tablespoon

METHOD

1. First of all, mix sausage slices, maple syrup, apricot preserves, and bourbon in a 1½ quart slow cooker.
2. Cover the crock pot lid and cook for about 4 hours.
3. Serve hot immediately.
4. If you want to serve later keep it in the cooker, you will have it warm for 1 hour in the cooker.
5. Use wooden toothpicks while serving.
6. Serve and enjoy.

Easy cooking tip: For easy cooking and cleaning, you can line the slow cooker with a disposable liner and after cooking transfer the food to the serving plate and dispose of the liner. In doing so, no sediments will stick on the cooker and will be easy to clean. Remember, do not serve the food with the disposable liner.

NUTRITIONAL VALUES

Calories: 86 | Total Fat: 2g | Carbohydrates: 7g | Protein: 8g | Cholesterol: 24mg | Calcium: 12mg | Sodium: 285mg | Potassium: 10mg

2. CROCK POT HOMEMADE MEATBALLS

Preparation time: 5 minutes | **Cooking time**: 4 hours | **Servings:** 8

INGREDIENTS

- Frozen meatballs – 1 Bag
- Ketchup – 1 Bottle (14 Ounces)
- Chili sauce – 1 Bottle (12 Ounces)
- Grape Jelly – 1 Jar
- Cooking oil – 2 tablespoon

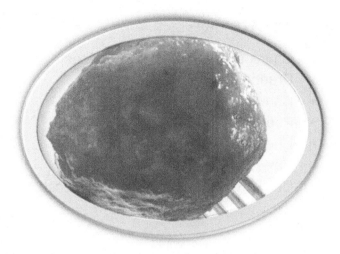

COOKING:

1. Grease a medium skillet and slow heat.
2. Put the meatballs and brown them evenly.
3. Once done, transfer all the meatballs to the crock pot.
4. Put all the ingredient on the meatballs.
5. Set your cooker for 4 hours cooking.
6. Check occasionally and stir it gently so that the sauce will spread on all the meatballs.
7. Serve hot.

Tips: You can also use baked meatballs instead of frozen, which can save your cooking time.

NUTRITIONAL VALUES

Calories: 322.9 | Carb: 11.6g | Fat: 25.6g | Cholesterol: 55.9g | Protein: 12.2g | Potassium: 19.5g

3. BUFFALO CHICKEN DIP

Preparation time: 10 minutes | **Cooking time:** 45 minutes | **Servings:** 20

INGREDIENTS

- Chunk chicken, dried - 10 ounces
- Cream cheese - 8 ounces
- Ranch dressing - 1 cup
- Pepper sauce - ¾ cup
- Cheddar cheese - 1½ cups
- Celery, clean and cut - 1 bunch
- Chicken flavored crackers - 8 ounces

METHOD

1. Take a skillet and heat chicken and sauce on medium temperature.
2. Add ranch dressing and cream cheese and stir well.
3. Now add half portion of the shredded cheese and continue stirring.
4. Transfer all these to a slow crock cooker.
5. Spread remaining cheese on top.
6. Cover and slow cook about 45 minutes until it becomes bubbly.
7. Serve hot with crackers and celery sticks.

Cooking tips: Use aluminum foil to keep the food moisture. It will also help to cook the food evenly and clean up the cooker easily.

NUTRITIONAL VALUES

Calories: 144 | Total Fat: 11.2g | Potassium: 27mg | Sodium: 349mg | Carbohydrate: 2.5g | Cholesterol: 0.36mg

4. SPINACH-ARTICHOKE DIP WITH BACON AND BLUE CHEESE

Preparation time: 25 minutes | **Cooking time: 4** hours | **Servings:** 24

INGREDIENTS

- Artichoke hearts, drained, chopped coarsely – 14 Ounces
- Bacon sliced – 4 Nos.
- Sweet onion, chopped coarsely – 1 Cup
- Frozen spinach, chopped, drained and thawed – 10 Ounces
- Red sweet pepper – 1 Cup
- Cream cheese – 8 Ounces
- Clove garlic, minced – 3 Nos.
- Blue cheese crumbled – 4 Ounces

- Dry mustard - ½ Teaspoon
- Light mayonnaise – 1 Cup
- Crackers, assorted

INSTRUCTIONS:

1. Take a medium skillet and cook bacon until it becomes crisp.
2. Drain it and crumble and set aside.
3. Pour 1 tablespoon bacon drippings and cook chopped onion for about 5 minutes, till it becomes tender.
4. In a 4-quart crock pot, mix onion, spinach, artichoke hearts, mayonnaise, red sweet pepper, blue cheese, cream cheese, dry mustard, and garlic.
5. Set to slow cooking for about 4 hours, until the cheese starts melting.
6. When the mixture become hot, add bacon.
7. It is ready and serves with assorted crackers.

Tips: You can use little oil at the time of cooking the bacon and use a paper towel to remove the oil. If you don't like assorted crackers, you can go for single type crackers of your choice.

NUTRITIONAL VALUES

Calories: 128 | Carb: 4g | Fat: 11g | Cholesterol: 22mg | Dietary fiber 2g | Sodium 341mg

5. MARSALA MUSHROOMS

Preparation time: 10 minutes | **Cooking time:** 8 hours | **Servings:** 8

INGREDIENTS

- Diced shallot - ⅓ cup
- Button mushrooms - 1½
- Fresh parsley, chopped - 2 tablespoons
- Finely chopped garlic - 2 cloves
- Chicken broth - ¼ cup
- Sweet Marsala - ¼ cup
- Cornstarch - 1 teaspoon
- Whipping cream, heavy - ½ cup
- Pepper - as required
- Salt to taste

- parmesan - optional
- Parsley additional - optional

METHOD

1. Grease the slow cooker with butter.
2. Place the mushrooms in the slow cooker.
3. Sprinkle garlic, parsley, and shallot.
4. Mix chicken broth and Marsala in a mixing bowl.
5. Transfer the mix over the mushrooms.
6. Drizzle pepper and salt.
7. Set the slow cooker for about 8 hours.
8. After 7 1/2 hours, mix heavy cream and cornstarch. Make sure to dissolve the cornstarch in the cream.
9. Slowly transfer the mix to the slow cooker and continue cooking.
10. You can season it with the optional ingredients.
11. Serve with bread or with toothpicks.

Cooking tips: Instead of shallot, you can use onion, if you don't like the flavor.

NUTRITIONAL VALUES

Calories: 101 | Total Fat: 8g | Cholesterol: 25mg | Sodium: 358mg | Carbohydrate: 4g | Protein: 2g

6. LOW CARB BUFFALO CHICKEN MEATBALLS APPETIZER

Preparation time: 20 minutes | **Cooking time:** 3 Hours and 20 Minutes | **Servings:** 16 Meatballs

INGREDIENTS

For Chicken Meatballs:

- Chicken, ground – 1 Pound
- Egg, whisked – 1
- Cayenne pepper - ¼ Teaspoon
- Breadcrumbs, gluten-free - ½ Cup
- Blue cheese for dressing - ½ Cup
- Salt - ½ Teaspoon

For Buffalo Sauce:

- Hot sauce - ½ Cup
- Butter, melted - ¼ Cup
- Clove garlic – 1
- Sour cream – 2 Tablespoon
- Salt - ¼ Teaspoon

DIRECTIONS:

Buffalo sauce:

1. Combine butter, hot sauce, garlic, sour cream and ¼ teaspoon salt and make a smooth sauce.

Chicken Meatballs:

2. Whisk egg, chicken, ½ teaspoon salt, breadcrumbs, cayenne pepper in a large bowl. Combine it by hand and mix properly.
3. Roll the mixture to form meatballs. Don't make too large balls.
4. Now in a 6-quart crockpot, pour a half portion of the buffalo sauce.
5. Place meatballs in a single layer in the bottom of the cooker.
6. Pour the remaining buffalo sauce over the meatballs.
7. Set the cooker for 4 hours.

8. It will be ready after 4 hours, just turn off it and allow it to settle.
9. Dress it with blue cheese and serve hot.

Tips: You can buy ready-made buffalo sauce, which will help you to save cooking effort. After using, keep the sauce in the fridge so that you can use for next time.

NUTRITIONAL VALUE:

Cal: 82 | Carb: 1g | Fat: 5g | Cholesterol: 43g | Sodium: 349mg | Potassium: 168mg

7. HOT WING DIP

Preparation time: 10 minutes | **Cooking time:** 3 hours | **Servings:** 10

INGREDIENTS

- Cream cheese (Low fat), cut up - 8 ounces
- Bottled Buffalo wing sauce - ½ cup
- Salad dressing blue cheese (low calorie) - 1½ tablespoons
- Chicken breast (cooked & chopped) - 1 cup
- Celery (finely chopped) – 1 stalk (½ cup)
- Fresh jalapeno chili pepper, seeded and minced - 1
- Celery, crosswise halved - 20 stalks

METHOD:

1. In a slow cooker mix cream cheese, chicken, wing sauce, dressing, jalapeno pepper and chopped celery.
2. Cover the crock pot lid and cook on low heat for three to four hours.
3. If you are using a slow cooker, set it for 4 hours, otherwise, cook for 2 hours
4. Serve the dish with celery pieces and enjoy.

Tips: If you love to have some crunch, add some crispy fried onions toward the end of the cooking session.

NUTRITIONAL VALUES

Calories: 99 | Total Fat: 7g | Cholesterol: 29g | Sodium: 168g | Carbohydrate 3g | Protein: 7g

8. CROCK POT TURKEY WITH CHERRY SAUCE APPETIZER

Preparation time: 20 minutes | **Cooking time:** 8 hours | **Servings:** 6

INGREDIENTS

- Turkey thighs – 4 Nos. (4 pounds approximately)
- Paprika, Spanish – 1 Teaspoon
- Cumin, grounded – 1 Teaspoon
- Chili powder – 1 Teaspoon
- Olive oil – 1 Tablespoon
- Onion – 1 No.
- Cinnamon - ½ Teaspoon
- Green apple – 2 Nos.
- Ketchup sauce – 1 Bottle
- Pomegranate seeds - 1½ Cups

- Salt to taste

INSTRUCTIONS:

1. Take a medium bowl and mix paprika, cumin, chili powder, cinnamon, and salt.
2. Rub olive oil on the turkey thighs, and then spread the spice mixture on the turkey.
3. Slice the onion and also slice the apple into wedges and place in the slow crockpot cooker.
4. Place the turkey on the top of apple and onion.
5. Pour half of the ketchup over the turkey.
6. Turn on the slow cooker for about 8 hours.
7. Once done, remove the turkey for cooling.
8. After cooling, by using two forks, shred the turkey thighs and put the serving dish.
9. Cut the remaining apple into the small pieces and mix with pomegranate seeds and spread over the turkey.
10. Toss with ketchup.

Tips: You can use this as an appetizer and also use as a filler for a sandwich. Instead of ketchup for tossing, you may also try using hot spice, if you wish to have a tangy taste.

NUTRITIONAL VALUES

Calories: 1047 | Carbs: 12.4g | Fat: 5.5g | Protein: 31.4g | Cholesterol: 73mg | Sodium: 84mg

9. CROCK POT RANCH MUSHROOMS APPETIZER

Preparation time: 15 minutes | **Cooking time:** 3 hours | **Servings: 18**

INGREDIENTS

- Washed mushrooms – 8 Ounces
- Dry salad dressing mix – 2.8 Ounces
- Ranch dressing mix – 1 Ounce
- Butter, melted - ½ cup

INSTRUCTIONS:

1. In a medium bowl, mix the butter thoroughly with ranch and dry salad dressing.
2. On a 4-quart crockpot cooker, place the mushrooms.
3. Pour butter mixture over it.
4. Close and cook on low heat about 3-4 hours.
5. Stir intermittently and check the cooking.
6. Serve hot

Tips: You can add fresh vegetables to make it healthier.

NUTRITIONAL VALUES

Calories: 85 | Carb: 7g | Fat: 6g | Cholesterol: 14mg | Dietary Fiber: 1g | Protein: 3g | Sodium: 89mg

10. LOW CARB CROCK POT SPINACH DIP

Preparation time: 10 minutes | **Cooking time:** 3 Hours and 30 Minutes | **Servings:** 3

INGREDIENTS

- Mozzarella cheese, shredded – 1 Cup
- Neufchatel cheese, cubed – 6 Ounces
- Parmesan cheese, grated - ¼ Cup
- Clove garlic, minced – 1
- Spinach leaves, fresh, chopped – 8 Ounces
- Artichoke hearts, washed, drained, chopped – 14 Ounces
- Black pepper, grounded - ¼ Teaspoon
- Salt to taste

INSTRUCTIONS:

1. In a 4-quart crockpot cooker, put all the ingredients.
2. Cover and set cooking slowly for about 3 hours.
3. Check occasionally and stir.
4. When it is hot and bubbly, continue cooking for another 30 minutes.
5. Serve hot.

Tips: The recipe is suitable to use with canned artichoke hearts. If you like a spicy dish, you can slightly increase the clove garlic to 2 or 3. Similarly, if you want to have greenish spinach, you can keep half portion of spinach and add in between the cooking.

NUTRITIONAL VALUE

Cal: 87 | Carb: 4g | Fat: 6g | Fiber: 1.6g | Protein: 5.2g | Cholesterol: 20mg | Sodium: 196mg

11. THAI CHICKEN WINGS WITH PEANUT SAUCE

Preparation time: 25 minutes | **Cooking time:** 5-6 hours (low) | **Servings:** 16

INGREDIENTS

- Chicken wing drummettes - 24 (about 2¼ pounds)
- Water - ¼ cup
- Lime juice - 1 tablespoon
- Ginger grounded - ¼ teaspoon
- Peanut Sauce – Check the recipe

METHOD

1. First of all, place chicken in a 3-4 quart slow cooker.
2. Add water, lime juice, and ginger to cooker.
3. Cover and cook on low heat for about 5 to 6 hours, if you cook on high temperature, just cook for about 2½ to 3 hours.
4. Prepare peanut sauce as per instruction.
5. Drain chicken very well. Use cooking liquid.
6. Paste half of the peanut sauce on chicken.
7. Keep warm and serve immediately.

PEANUT SAUCE INGREDIENTS

- Peanut butter cream - ½ cup
- Water - ½ cup
- Sodium soy sauce – 2 tablespoons
- Garlic, minced – 2 cloves
- Ginger, grounded - ½ teaspoon
- Crushed red pepper - ¼ teaspoon

METHOD

1. Mix the peanut butter, soy sauce, water, garlic, mashed red pepper, and ginger.
2. Heat over low until the mixture becomes smooth about one cup.

Speed cooking tips: Instead of using slow cooker, try to use instant pot cooker, which can reduce your cooking efforts.

Peanut paste consistency: Add hot water to manage the sauce consistency.

NUTRITIONAL VALUES: Calories: 106 | Total Fat: 6g | Cholesterol: 15mg | Sodium: 159mg | Carbohydrate: 3 g | Fiber: 1g | Protein: 9g

12. SPICY CAPONATA

Preparation time: 45 minutes | **Cooking time:** 5 hours | **Servings:** 32

INGREDIENTS

- Tomatoes, chopped coarsely - 1 pound
- Eggplant - 2 (cut into ¾ inches size)
- Celery stalks, sliced: 1⅓ cups
- Zucchini, cut into half lengthwise and then crosswise - 2 cups
- Red bell pepper, 1-inch size - 1
- Sweet onion chopped - 1 cup
- Raisins - ½ cup
- Sugar - 1 tablespoon
- Tomato paste - 3 tablespoon
- Ground pepper - ½ teaspoon
- Red pepper cracked - 1 teaspoon
- Basil leaves, fresh - ¼ cup

- Italian parsley fresh, chopped - ¼ cup
- Green olives, coarsely chopped - ¼ cup
- Drained capers - ¼ cup
- Vinegar, red wine - 2 tablespoon

METHOD:

1. Take a 6-quart slow cooker and spray with cooking oil.
2. Mix tomatoes, eggplant, bell pepper, raisins, onion, zucchini, celery, cracked pepper, sugar and pepper in the cooker.
3. Cover and cook on low heat about 5 hours
4. Mix parsley, basil, capers, olive and vinegar and add to the cooker.
5. Let it settle and cool.
6. After that keep in the fridge until get cooled adequately.
7. Serve the Caponata cold with crackers or bread.

Flavor: Try using Sicilian flavors for a change.

Serving: You can serve it at room temperature instead of chilled.

NUTRITIONAL VALUES

Calories: 25 | Total Fat: 0g | Sodium 60mg | Carbohydrates: 5g | Fiber: 1g | Protein: 1g

KETO CROCK POT
MAIN DISH

1. CHILI PULLED PORK TACOS

Preparation time: 10-15 minutes | **Cooking time**: 8 hours | **Serves**: 10

INGREDIENTS:

- Pork meet butt or shoulder - 4½ pounds
- Cumin grounded - 1½ teaspoon
- Chili powder - 2 tablespoon
- Oregano grounded - ½ teaspoon
- Broth - ½ cup
- Red pepper flakes - ¼ teaspoon
- Bay leaf - 1
- Grounded cloves - a pinch
- Salt to taste

METHOD

1. Combine salt, oregano, chili powder, cumin, cloves and pepper flakes in medium bowl.
2. Clean the pork and rub the spice mixture on the pork meet.
3. Keep it in the fridge for about 2 hours and let it get marinated properly.
4. Now keep ready your crock pot slow cooker and put the marinated meet to it.
5. Add the broth and bay leaf.
6. Cook it about 8 hours by setting on slow cooking.
7. Once cooking is over, place the cooked meet on a cutting board and by using two fork, and shred the meat.
8. Serve it hot.

Cooking tips: You can reduce the marinating time by just keeping it for an hour or so.

Serving tips: You can serve it along with lettuce wrap, cilantro leaves, avocado slices and hot sauce.

NUTRITIONAL VALUES

Calories: 159.8 | Fat: 7g | Carbohydrate: 2.7g | Dietary Fiber: 2.6g | Protein: 20.6g

2. CROCK POT BALSAMIC BONELESS CHICKEN THIGHS

Preparation time: 5 minutes | **Cooking time**: 4 hours | **Servings**: 8

INGREDIENTS:

- Ground garlic -1 teaspoon
- Basil dried - 1 teaspoon
- Salt - ½ teaspoon
- Pepper - ½ teaspoon
- Onion, dried & minced - 2 teaspoons
- Minced garlic cloves - 4
- Olive oil, extra virgin - 1 tablespoon
- Balsamic vinegar - ½ cup
- Chicken thighs boneless and skinless - 8 (about 24 ounces)
- Fresh chopped parsley

METHOD:

1. Take a medium bowl and mix the all dry spices and paste all over the chicken.
2. Pour one tablespoon olive oil to the crock pot.
3. Add garlic.
4. Place the chicken.
5. You can dispense the balsamic vinegar on the chicken and make sure it reaches everywhere on the chicken.
6. Cover the crock pot and cook on high about 4 hours.
7. Once cooking over, transfer the dish to a serving bowl.
8. Sprinkle fresh parsley on top the chicken.
9. Serve and enjoy.

Quick cooking tips: Use instant pot cooker, which will reduce your cooking time. Try adding potatoes or fresh vegetables to give a vegetable twist for the dish.

NUTRITIONAL VALUES

Calories: 133 | Total Fat: 4 g | Cholesterol: 85 mg | Sodium: 832 mg | Total Carbohydrates: 5.6 g | Dietary Fiber: 0.1 g | Protein: 20.1g

3. CROCK POT CHILE VERDE

Preparation time: 15 minutes | **Cooking time:** 8 hours | **Servings:** 9

INGREDIENTS:

- Boneless chicken - 2 pound
- Butter - 3 tablespoon
- Cilantro, fine chopped - 3 tablespoon
- Salsa Verde - 1½ cups
- Minced clove garlic - 5
- Cilantro for garnishing - 1 tablespoon
- Salt to taste

COOKING METHOD:

1. Turn on the crock pot and put two tablespoon of butter and let it melt.
2. Add 2 tablespoon cilantro and 4 minced garlic to the crock pot and stir.
3. Now take large fry pan and heat on medium high temperature and put 1 tablespoon of butter.
4. Add 1 tablespoon cilantro and minced 1 tablespoon minced garlic.
5. Now add the pork meat to the frying pan and let it brown sears on all side.
6. After meat brown sears all side, transfer the meat, cilantro, butter and garlic to the crock pot.
7. Add the salsa Verde into the crock pot and stir properly.
8. Set the slow cooker for 8 hours and continue cooking.
9. Serve over cauliflower rice or serve in lettuce cups.

Tips for fast cooking: Using instant pot cooker can considerably reduce the cooking time.

NUTRITIONAL VALUES

Protein: 29g | Fat: 23g | Carbohydrates: 2.4g | Fibers: 0.6g

4. KETO LAMB BARBACOA

Preparation time: 10 minutes | **Cooking time:** 6 hours | **Servings:** 10

INGREDIENTS

- Boneless leg of lamb – 5½ pounds
- Dried mustard - ¼ cup
- Himalayan salt - 2 tablespoons
- Smoked paprika - 2 tablespoons
- Grounded cumin - 1 tablespoon
- Dried oregano - 1 tablespoon
- Chipotle powder - 1 tablespoon
- Water - 1 cup

METHOD

1. Take a small mixing bowl and add oregano, salt, paprika, cumin and chipotle powder and mix everything properly.
2. Now coat the lamb with mustard and spread the spice you mixed in the bowl evenly on the lamb.
3. Place the marinated lamb in a slow cooker and add water to it.
4. Let it cook for six hours.
5. Shred the lamb with a fork after cooking
6. Leave only one cup of water in the lamb and drain out the rest of water.

Fast cooking tips: Cook the lamb in an instant cooker or pressure cooker without adding water. Set the timer to 65. After finished cooking, just wait for another 10-15 minutes by that time the steam pressure will settle by itself. Then you can continue with the remaining cooking process. Using this method can save 4 hours.

NUTRITIONAL VALUES

Calories: 492 | Carbohydrates: 1.2 g | Fats: 36 g | Potassium: 35 mg | Sodium: 702 mg | Protein: 38 g | Dietary Fiber: 0.2 g

5. CROCK POT CHICKEN SOUP KALE

Preparation time: 45 minutes | **Cooking time:** 6 hours | **Servings:** 8

INGREDIENTS

- Chicken Thighs - 2 pounds (about 5 thighs)
- Salt – 1 or ½ tablespoon
- Pepper - 1 tablespoon
- Fresh Thyme - 2
- Garlic - 2 cloves
- Chicken Stock - 5 cups
- Chicken Base - 2 tablespoons
- Carrots - 1 pound (sliced in halfway)
- Yellow Onion - 1
- Chopped Bunch Kale - 1

- Fresh Thyme - ½ tablespoon
- Salt according to your taste

COOKING METHOD

1. First of all, place the chicken thighs on the base of the crock pot and sprinkle the salt and pepper over it.
2. Put the thyme and garlic over the layer of chicken.
3. Pour water into the pot. Cook the chicken for four hours.
4. Transfer the chicken to a bowl after cooking and remove the thyme from the pot.
5. Again add chicken to the crock pot and put it on the flame.
6. Add carrots, onions and chopped thyme to the chicken and cook for 2 hours.
7. Add Kale after 90 minutes.
8. Remove the bones from the soup.
9. Add seasonings or salt and pepper.

Tips for fast cooking: To reduce the cooking time, you can use instant broth recipes and instant pot cook. Also, using a pressure cooker is an excellent option, just allow it blow whistle 5-6 time and do the remaining cooking process.

NUTRITIONAL VALUES

Calories: 317 | Cholesterol: 115mg | Sodium: 745mg | Potassium: 480mg | Protein: 22g | Carbohydrates: 8g | Fat 20g

6. LOW CARB CROCK POT SHORT BEEF RIBS

Preparation time: 15 minutes | **Cooking Time:** 4 hours | **Servings:** 12

INGREDIENTS

- Beef with short ribs or boneless – 4 pounds
- Onion, chopped – 1.5 cups
- Beef broth – 1 cup
- Olive oil – 2 tablespoons
- Worcestershire sauce or ordinary homemade – 2 tablespoons
- Tomato paste – 2 tablespoons
- Garlic clove, minced – 3 Nos.
- Salt to taste
- Pepper to taste

- Red wine – 1.5 cup
- Celery, carrots - optional

METHOD

1. In a large skillet, pour oil and heat on medium temperature.
2. Season the ribs, one side with salt and pepper.
3. Put half of the ribs, facing the seasoned into the hot oil.
4. Flip it once the side becomes brown.
5. Remove and set aside.
6. Continue the remaining.
7. Take a 4-quart crockpot and place short ribs into it.
8. In the skillet put the remaining ingredients and boil it.
9. Cook until the onion becomes tender.
10. Transfer it to the crockpot.
11. Cover and continue cooking for 8-10 hours.

Tips: Add celery and carrots to the skillet and cook it along with remaining ingredients, if you want to have some more vegetable in the dish.

NUTRITIONAL VALUES

Calories: 489 | Carb: 3g | Fat: 42g | Protein: 16g | Cholesterol: 83mg | Sodium: 179mg | Potassium: 386mg

7. CROCK POT CHICKEN LO MEIN

Preparation time: 10 minutes | **Cooking time:** 4 hours | **Servings:** 6

INGREDIENTS

- Chicken sliced – 1½ Pounds
- Napa cabbage washed – 1 Bunch
- Low carb noodles – 12 Ounces
- Clove garlic, minced – 1 Teaspoon
- Salt to taste
- Pepper as required

<u>For marinating:</u>

- Tamari/soy aminos – 1 Tablespoon
- Garlic paste - ½ Teaspoon
- Sesame oil - ½ Teaspoon

<u>For making sauce:</u>

- Chicken broth - ¾ Cup
- Sweetener – 1 Tablespoon
- Tamari/Soy aminos - ¼ Cup
- Vinegar – 1 Tablespoon
- Sesame oil – 2 Teaspoons
- Pepper chili flakes – 1 Teaspoon
- Thickener (optional) - ½ teaspoon

METHOD

1. Marinate the chicken using the ingredients and keep it in the fridge for setting about 30 minutes. Use a small bowl to marinate.
2. Clean the crockpot and coat slightly with non-stick oil.
3. Put the marinated chicken in the cooker and start cooking in slow heat for about 2 hours.
4. Stir it intermittently and also check the tenderness of the chicken.
5. Once done, remove the chicken from the cooker and put garlic, ginger and vegetables into the cooker and place the cooked chicken on top of it.
6. Now it is time for making the sauce.
7. Mix all the sauce ingredients in a bowl and transfer everything to the cooker.
8. Continue cooking for about 2 hours and stir intermittently.
9. Ten minutes before winding up the cooking, rinse the noodle and keep it ready.

10. Transfer the washed and soaked noodles into the cooker.
11. Cover the noodles with the sauce by using tongs.
12. Add the thickener if required.
13. Just put the crockpot to a high temperature for about 15 minutes.
14. Serve hot

Tips: You can also try using boneless chicken or skinless thighs, as per your preferred choice. Similarly, you can use bok choy instead of napa cabbage. Adding any other low carb vegetable is an ideal option, so you can try using bell pepper or broccoli. The same method can also apply to other meats.

NUTRITIONAL VALUES

Calories: 174 | Carb: 3.1g | Fat: 10.2g | Protein: 24.5g | Sodium: 436mg | Dietary Fiber: 1.6g

8. SLOW COOKER CHICKEN & KALE SOUP

Preparation time: 5 minutes | **Cooking time:** 4 hours | **Servings:** 6 bowls

INGREDIENTS:

- Boneless chicken thighs (Skin removed) - 6
- Homemade chicken bone broth - 3½ cups
- White onion large chopped - ½ cup
- Garlic clove mashed - 4
- Shredded carrots - 1½ cups
- Chopped kale - 4 cups
- Parsley - 1½ tablespoon
- Salt and pepper to taste

METHOD

1. Place washed chicken in the slow cooker.
2. Layer with onions as your choice and add smashed garlic and broth.
3. Use homemade bone broth for yummy flavor.
4. You can remove the bones once the soup is ready.
5. Cook the chicken with the onions and garlic on low for 4 to 6 hours until the chicken starts to come apart.
6. Use a fork to separate into chunks.
7. Add carrots, kale, parsley and salt and pepper.
8. Cook for one hour.
9. Serve and enjoy.

Cooking tips: Using frozen chicken and also cooking by using instant pot cooker can reduce cooking time considerably.

NUTRITIONAL VALUES

Calories: 261 | Calories from Fat: 189 | Fat: 32% | Sodium: 11% | Carbohydrates: 1% | Protein: 28%

9. LOW CARB CROCK POT CABBAGE ROLLS

Preparation time: 10 minutes | **Cooking time:** 5 hours | **Servings:** 6

INGREDIENTS

- Cabbage leaves, large - 12
- Beef minced - 1 pound
- Parmesan cheese - 1 cup
- Garlic cloves finely minced - 2
- Onion powder - 1 teaspoon
- Fresh parsley, chopped, one small handful - 1
- Pepper - ½ teaspoon
- Marinara sauce sugarless- 1 cup

METHOD

1. First of all, cook the cabbage leaves slightly to make it soften. You can put the cabbage leaves in microwave until it become tender for about 2-3 minutes or you can boil it in the water for 3 minutes.
2. Place a ½ cup of the marinara sauce into the slow cooker.
3. Mix the meat by using mix bowl with parmesan, minced garlic, parsley and pepper.
4. Put ¼ cup of meat filling on each cabbage leaf.
5. Roll up each cabbage leaf looks like a burrito.
6. Place each cabbage roll into the slow cooker
7. Use the marinara sauce ½ cup on all the cabbage rolls.
8. Cook on high about 5 hours. On high temperature, you have to cook it about 2-3 hours.
9. Serve as per your choice.

Cooking tip: You can cook this dish in a Dutch oven if you are not using a crock pot. When using a Dutch oven, do the cooking in slow heat and cover the oven, until the cabbage becomes tender.

NUTRITIONAL VALUES

Calories: 175.4 | Fat: 8.1g | Cholesterol: 40mg | Sodium: 113.6mg | Potassium: 104.8mg | Carbohydrates: 9.4g | Protein: 13.6g

10. PORK ROAST WITH SUGARLESS CHIMICHURRI SAUCE

Preparation time: 30 minutes | **Cooking time:** 6 hours | **Servings:** 12

INGREDIENTS

- Pork Roast boneless - 3 pounds
- Extra Virgin Olive Oil - 4 tablespoons
- Carrots trimmed and quartered lengthwise -1 Pound
- Sweet Onion thickly sliced -1
- Real Salt to taste
- Chimichurri sauce (Prepare as per the recipe)

METHOD

1. Place the pork roast in a pot. Add 2 tablespoons of the olive oil over the roast and sprinkle it with salt and pepper.
2. Cover and cook on high for 6 hours. In slow cooking, cook it about 12 hours.
3. After 4 hours of cooking, add the onions and carrots around the roast.
4. Cook the roast, carrots, and onions for 2 hours until you can easily pull apart the pork and the carrots become soft.
5. Place the roast, carrots, and onions on serving platter and drizzle with sauce.
6. Serve with extra sauce as per you like.

INGREDIENTS FOR CHIMICHURRI SAUCE

- Basil leaves fresh – 1 cup
- Garlic clove – 3
- Lemon juice – 2 tablespoons
- Olive oil, extra virgin - ½ cup
- Black pepper - ¼ teaspoon
- Cayenne pepper - ¼ teaspoon
- Salt – 1 teaspoon

METHOD

1. In a food processor, combine all the ingredients.
2. Continue blending until the basil becomes small and even.
3. Your sauce is ready to sprinkle on the dish.

Tips: As a quick way of cooking, you can fry the onion and carrot in a pan by using the remaining 2 tablespoons of olive oil, until it begins to caramelize. Then add it to the crock roast pot.

NUTRITIONAL VALUES

Calories: 167 | Total Fat: 8g | Carbohydrates: 5g | Cholesterol: 47mg | Sodium: 65mg | Potassium: 436mg | Protein: 17g

11. SLOW COOKER MOSCOW CHICKEN

Preparation time: 10-15 minutes | **Cooking time**: 6 hours | **Servings**: 6

INGREDIENTS:

- Chicken thighs - 6
- Grated ginger - ½ teaspoon
- Bacon, sliced - 6
- Russian salad dressing - 10 ounces
- Clove garlic, chopped - 2
- Onion, chopped - 2
- Pepper as required
- Salt to taste

METHOD:

1. Take a large skillet and heat on medium temperature.
2. Put chicken and cook it until both sides become brown.
3. Let it cool after done.
4. Now wrap the chicken thighs in bacon and put it into the slow cooker.
5. Spread ginger and garlic over the chicken.
6. Top it with Russian salad
7. Cook for 5-6 hours
8. Once ready, season it with pepper and salt.

Cooking tips: Use a baking liner cloth in the cooker for easy cleaning.

NUTRITIONAL FACTS

Calories: 150.7 | Total Fat: 2.8g | Sodium: 362.9mg | Cholesterol: 57.3mg | Potassium: 275.7mg | Carbohydrates: 10.5g | Dietary Fiber: 1.8g | Protein: 14.9g

12. MEXICAN CROCK POT BEEF ROAST

Preparation time: 15 minutes | **Cooking time**: 7 hours | **Servings**: 10

INGREDIENTS:

- Beef chuck arm – 3½ Pounds
- Cumin, grounded – 1 Teaspoon
- Garlic, minced – 2 Teaspoons
- Black pepper, grounded – 1 Teaspoon
- Tomato paste – 2 Tablespoons
- Coriander, grounded - ½ Teaspoon
- Fresh salsa – 2 Cups
- Bacon grease – 3 Tablespoons
- Beef broth – 2 Cups

- Sauce – 2 Tablespoons
- Salt to taste

INSTRUCTIONS:

1. Season the beef with grounded black pepper and spices.
2. Take a heavy skillet and over medium-high heat, melt the bacon grease.
3. Roast it until becoming brown on all sides.
4. Put all the roasted beef in the crock pot.
5. Add tomato paste, sauce and salsa over the meet.
6. Add beef broth.
7. Put the remaining bacon grease and any other leftovers over the beef.
8. Cover and cook on low heat.
9. Depending on the meet, you need to cook it for 6-8 hours on slow cooking.
10. Once the cooking is over, remove the beef to a large bowl and pull the meat into small rags, when it is cool. You can do it by hand or with forks. Remove excess fat if anything is there.
11. Once done, serve hot.

Tips: While serving, you can add some spicy cream for a different taste. Also, to soften the salsa, run it in a blender and transfer for cooking.

NUTRITIONAL VALUES

Calories: 608 | Carb: 7g | Fat: 36g | Protein: 44g | Dietary Fiber: 6g

KETO CROCK POT
SIDE DISH

1. CROCK POT FRESH GREEN BEANS

Preparation time: 20 minutes | **Cooking time:** 1-2 hours | **Servings:** 4

INGREDIENTS

- Bacon, chopped – 6 Slices
- Onions, minced - ½ Cups
- Garlic, minced – 1 Teaspoon
- Fresh green beans, 1 Pound
- Water – 1 Cup
- Black pepper, grounded – 1 Pinch
- Salt to taste

COOKING INSTRUCTIONS:

1. Put onions, garlic, and salt in a medium skillet and cook on medium heat until it becomes tender.
2. Now transfer all these to your crock pot and place the chopped fresh beans and bacon over it.
3. Add water.
4. Add salt if required.
5. Close the crockpot and set on low cooking for about 2 hours.
6. Check intermittently and stir.
7. After cooking done, season with pepper.
8. Serve hot.

Tip: Transfer the cooked food to your serving dish and cover it with aluminum foil paper for keeping it warm.

NUTRITIONAL VALUE

Calories: 97 | Carb: 7g | Cholesterol: 14mg | Protein: 6.2g | Sodium: 343mg

2. SLOW COOKER MUSHROOM SAUTÉ

Preparation time: 5 minutes | **Baking time:** 1.30 hours | **Servings:** 4

INGREDIENTS

- Button mushrooms, sliced – 1 Pound
- Butter – 1 Tablespoon
- Olive oil - ½ Tablespoon
- Balsamic vinegar - ½ Tablespoon
- Oregano, dried - ⅛ Tablespoon
- Clove garlic, minced – 1
- Water - ¼ cup
- Salt to taste
- Pepper to taste

INSTRUCTIONS:

1. In a large skillet, melt butter with olive oil.
2. Add water, mushroom, garlic, oregano, vinegar, salt and sauté for about 5 minutes.
3. Then transfer all these to your slow cooker.
4. Set slow cooking for about 1.30 hours, until mushroom becomes tender.
5. Stir occasionally.
6. Serve hot.

Tips: You can add the fresh vegetable to make it healthier. Add one tomato, if you like to have gravy for the dish.

NUTRITIONAL VALUE

Calories: 94 | Carb: 5.3g | Cholesterol: 15mg | Protein: 2.3g | Sodium: 46mg

3. CROCK POT CAULIFLOWER SIDE DISH

Preparation time: 20 minutes | **Cooking time:** 1.30-2 Hours | **Servings:** 12

INGREDIENTS

- Fresh cauliflower – 16 Ounces
- Sour cream – 8 Ounces
- Chicken bouillon granules – 3 Teaspoon
- Cheddar cheese - 1½ Cups
- Butter, cubed - ¼ Cup
- Stuffing mix – 1 Cup
- Mustard, grounded – 1 Teaspoon
- Walnuts, chopped - ¾ Cup
- Salt to taste

INSTRUCTIONS:

1. Clean the cauliflower, wash and dry and keep aside
2. In a large bowl, put bouillon, sour cream, mustard and mix entirely.
3. Add cauliflower and mix the ingredients properly.
4. Transfer the mix to your crock pot and set low cooking for about 2 hours.
5. Stir occasionally.
6. Once cooking is over, transfer it to a serving dish.
7. Take a large skillet and heat butter.
8. Add walnut and stuffing mix and toast it slightly and spread over the cooked food.
9. Serve hot.

Tips: You can also use frozen cauliflower, but look for the instructions to use. It is also good to season the dish as per your choice.

INGREDIENTS:

Calories: 276 | Carb: 9.7g | Fat: 18g | Cholesterol: 57mg | Protein: 10g | Fiber: 3g

4. CROCK POT ZUCCHINI TOMATO CASSEROLE

Preparation time: 10 minutes | **Cooking time:** 1.30-2 Hours | **Servings:** 8

INGREDIENTS

- Zucchini, medium size, diced – 6 Cups
- Butter, melted – 4 Tablespoons
- Tomatoes, medium size – 2 Nos.
- Breadcrumbs, soft – 1 Cup
- Egg, beaten – 1 Nos.
- Onion, minced – 2 Tablespoons
- Cheddar cheese – 1 Cup
- Fresh parsley, minced – 3 Tablespoons
- Fresh basil, minced – 1 Tablespoon

- Cheese, processed – 1 Cup
- Garlic powder - ½ Teaspoon
- Salt to taste
- Pepper to taste

INSTRUCTIONS:

1. Sauté zucchini in a skillet by adding 2 tablespoons of butter until it becomes crisp.
2. Drain it and keep aside.
3. Now take a bowl and mix all the remaining ingredients.
4. Add the cooked zucchini and butter.
5. Transfer the mix to the crockpot and set low cooking for about 1.30 – 2 hours.
6. Check occasionally and stir.
7. Serve hot or after settling.

Tips: For a variation, it will be a good practice using dried parsley instead of fresh. Similarly, you can make use of dried basil instead of fresh. It won't make significant changes in the nutritional content. In the event, if you are unable to get fresh basil and parsley, you can try these options.

NUTRITIONAL VALUE:

Calories: 224 | Carb: 8g | Fat: 16g | Cholesterol: 90mg | Sodium: 527mg | Fiber: 2g | Protein: 10g

5. CREAMY PARMESAN SPINACH SIDE DISH

Preparation time: 30 minutes | **Cooking time:** 2-3 hours | **Servings:** 12

INGREDIENTS

- Baby spinach – 9 Ounces
- Red onion, chopped – 1 No.
- Butter – 1 Tablespoon
- Cheese, cubed – 8 Ounces
- Half and half cream - ½ Cup
- Sour cream – 8 Ounces
- Clove garlic – 3 Nos.
- Parmesan cheese, grated – 3 Tablespoons
- Artichoke hearts, rinsed, drained, chopped – 14 Ounces
- Fresh dill – 1 Tablespoon

- Crackers – 8 Nos.
- Salt to taste
- Pepper to taste

INSTRUCTIONS:

1. Wash spinach, dry and keep aside.
2. Take a large saucepan and sauté onion until it becomes tender.
3. In low heat add cream cheese, half-and-half, sour cream, ⅓ parmesan cheese, pepper, and garlic.
4. Continue cooking until the cheese starts melting.
5. Add artichokes, spinach, dill, and salt.
6. Now transfer all the mix to the crockpot.
7. Set low cooking and continue for 2-3 hours.
8. Once done, add remaining parmesan cheese and cracker crumbs.
9. Serve medium hot.

Tips: You can buy crackers as per your choice of flavors. If baby spinach is not available, you can use the available one, and you need to manage the cooking time to match the ingredient quality.

NUTRITIONAL VALUES

Calories: 196 | Carb: 9.7g | Fat: 14g | Protein: 7g | Fiber: 2g | Sodium: 394mg

6. CHICKEN CAULIFLOWER SIDE DISH

Preparation time: 15 minutes | **Cooking time:** 6 hours | **Servings:** 4

INGREDIENTS

- Cooked chicken, diced – 2 Cups
- Cauliflower rice – 2 Cups
- Italian seasoning – 1 Tablespoon
- Mushroom, chopped – 2 Cups
- Parmesan and Garlic cheese - ½ Cups
- Whipping cream - ¼ Cups
- Egg white – 4
- Mozzarella cheese (Optional)

INSTRUCTIONS:

1. Combine cauliflower rice, mushrooms, chicken and Italian seasoning.
2. Transfer the mix to 4-quart crockpot.
3. Take another bowl and mix egg white, parmesan, and cheese.
4. Pour the mix over the cauliflower mix in the crockpot.
5. Set the slow crockpot for 6 hours cooking.
6. Check occasionally.
7. Serve cold and top with mozzarella, optional.

Tips: Topping with mozzarella is optional. You can alternatively use any other desired topping. Check occasionally to make sure the dish has enough water content for proper cooking. It is better to keep ready some water, and add if and when required.

NUTRITIONAL VALUES

Calories: 72.5 | Carb: 7.1g | Fat: 3.8g | Cholesterol: 9.3mg | Potassium: 78.5mg | Sodium: 180.5mg | Protein: 3.5g

7. CROCK POT GREEN BEAN CASSEROLE

Preparation time: 15 minutes | **Cooking time: 4** hours | **Servings:** 8

INGREDIENTS:

- Green beans, cooked – 1 Pound
- Bacon, cooked & chopped - ⅓ Pound

For Creamy Cheese Sauce:

- Onion, finely minced – 3 Ounces
- Clove garlic, minced – 1
- Dry vermouth – 4 Tablespoons
- Parsley, minced – 1 Tablespoon
- Lemon zest – 1 Teaspoon
- Bacon drippings – 2 Tablespoons
- Cream cheese – 6 Ounces
- Chicken broth - ¾ Cup
- Cheddar cheese, grated – 3 Ounces
- Worcestershire sauce – 1 Teaspoon
- Salt to taste
- Pepper to taste

For Topping:

- Low carb bread crumbs - ⅓ Cups
- Garlic, granulated - ⅛ Teaspoons
- Salt to taste
- Olive oil – 2 Teaspoon (Use as required)

INSTRUCTION:

1. In a small skillet cook beans and bacon by adding little water and after cooking drain and set aside.
2. Medium heat a large skillet and add little bacon drippings.
3. Add the minced onion and stir until it becomes translucent.
4. Then add garlic and continue stirring until it becomes soft.
5. Slow down the heat and add parsley, wine and lemon zest.
6. Continue stirring for some time until the smell of the wine disappears.
7. Now add the cream cheese and let it melt. Stir occasionally.
8. Add chicken broth slowly and sauté occasionally.
9. Add cheddar cheese, mustard, Worcestershire sauce, pepper and salt and continue stirring.

10. Transfer the mixture to the bowl of bacon and beans.
11. Mix it properly.
12. Transfer the entire mixture to the crockpot and set for low cooking about 4 hours.
13. Make the topping. For that put the breadcrumbs into a small bowl. Add granulated garlic and salt as required along with olive oil as needed. Mix it properly and sprinkle on top of the dish.
14. Check the dish occasionally and make sure that there is enough water for cooking. If it looks dry, you can add some water or chicken broth.
15. Serve hot.

Tips: Instead of dry vermouth, you can use white wine. For topping, you can try using pork rinds, if you are not comfortable with breadcrumbs.

NUTRITIONAL VALUES

Calories: 300 | Carb: 6g | Fat: 18g | Protein: 12g | Cholesterol: 54mg | Sodium: 776mg | Potassium: 272mg

8. SLOW COOKED CROCK POT BROCCOLI

Preparation time: 10 minutes | **Cooking time:** 4 hours | **Servings:** 10

INGREDIENTS

- Broccoli, frozen, chopped – 6 Cups
- Cheddar cheese, grated - 1½ Cups
- Condensed cream of celery soup - 10¾ Ounces
- Onion, chopped - ¼ Cup
- Worcestershire sauce - ½ Teaspoon
- Pepper to taste
- Crackers, butter flavored – 1 Cup
- Butter – 2 Tablespoon

INSTRUCTIONS:

1. Combine broccoli, onion, 1 cup cheese, soup, Worcestershire sauce and add pepper to taste in a large bowl.
2. Grease the bottom of crockpot.
3. Transfer the mixture to the crockpot.
4. Spread the crackers on top and spread the butter.
5. Cover and cook for about 4 hours.
6. Once done, sprinkle the remaining cheese.
7. Continue cooking for another 10-15 minutes until the cheese starts to melt.
8. Serve hot.

Tips: You can also try using fresh broccoli which required more time for cooking. Similarly, you can choose the flavors of crackers as per your preference. It would be a good idea to try different flavors when making the dish on a regular basis.

NUTRITIONAL VALUE

Cal: 159 | Carb: 9g | Fat: 11g | Fiber: 1g | Cholesterol: 25mg | Sodium: 431mg

9. BALSAMIC GLAZED BRUSSELS SPROUTS

Preparation: 15-20 minutes | **Cooking:** 5-6 hours | **Serve:** 6

INGREDIENTS:

- Brussels sprout - 2 pound
- Chicken broth - 2 cups
- Balsamic glaze - 2 tablespoons
- Extra virgin olive oil - 2 tablespoon
- Roasted pine nuts - ¼ cups
- Parmesan cheese grated - ¼ cups
- Salt to taste
- Pepper as required

METHOD

1. Wash and trim out the head portion of brussels
2. Cut the brussels in half.
3. Put the brussels into a slow cooker.
4. Add ½ teaspoon salt.
5. Cover and cook on low heat for about 5-6 hours.
6. Transfer the cooked brussels to the serving dish.
7. Garnish with pepper and salt.
8. Spread balsamic glaze.
9. Sprinkle the remaining olive oil and spread roasted pine nuts.
10. Dress with parmesan on top.
11. Serve hot.

Cooking tips: While selecting the vegetable or any other foodstuff for cooking try to use the fresh ones always. For fast cooking, you can use the instant cooker, which can reduce the cooking time considerably.

NUTRITIONAL VALUES

Carbs: 9.6g | Fiber: 3.5g | Fat: 0.3g | Cholesterol: 0.0mg | Protein: 3.2g | Potassium: 359.0mg | Sodium: 179.1mg

10. ITALIAN MUSHROOMS – CROCKPOT SIDE DISH

Preparation: 10 minutes | **Cooking:** 5 hours | **Serve:** 6

INGREDIENTS:

- Fresh mushrooms – 1 Pound
- Onion, sliced – 1 Large
- Butter, melted - ½ Cup
- Italian salad dressing mix – 1 Packet

INSTRUCTIONS:

1. Spread onion and mushrooms in a 4-quart crockpot cooker.
2. In a bowl mix salad dress and butter and pour on top of the vegetable in the pot.
3. Cover and pot.
4. Cook for about 5 hours.
5. Check occasionally to confirm the tenderness of the vegetable.
6. Serve hot.

Tips: Make sure to check the pot intermittently to confirm the tenderness of the vegetable. Overcooking may spoil the quality of the dish.

NUTRITIONAL VALUE

Cal: 99 | Carb: 6g | Cholesterol: 20mg | Protein: 3g | Fiber: 1g | Sodium: 281mg

11. GARLIC GREEN BEANS AND GORGONZOLA SIDE DISH

Preparation: 20 minutes | **Cooking:** 3 hours | **Serve:** 10

INGREDIENTS:

- Green beans, fresh, trimmed – 2 Pounds
- Gorgonzola cheese, crumbled - ¾ Cups
- Water chestnuts, sliced, drained – 8 Ounces
- Bacon strips, cooked & crumbled – 5 Nos.
- Onions, chopped, green - 4 Nos.
- Chicken broth - ⅓ Cups
- Thyme minced, fresh – 2 Tablespoons
- Clove garlic, minced – 4 Nos.
- Sour cream – 8 Ounces
- Salt to taste

PREPARATION:

1. Mix chicken broth, garlic, thyme in medium bowl.
2. Add salt to taste.
3. In a skillet roast bacon to become crisp and once done, crumble it.
4. In a 4-quart crockpot, place water chestnuts, green beans, green onions and ¼ cup cooked bacon.
5. Pour the mix of broth, garlic, and thyme over on top of the vegetable in the crockpot.
6. Cover the pot and cook for about 4 hours.
7. Check intermittently to confirm the tenderness of the beans.
8. Do not overcook. Once done, drain the water from the crockpot.
9. Before serving, add sour cream, and sprinkle cheese.
10. Sprinkle the remaining bacon.
11. Serve in medium hot.

Tips: Instead of chicken broth, you can also use white wine for a different taste. Also, you can try using dried thyme instead of fresh thyme in the same proportion.

NUTRITIONAL VALUE

Cal: 142 | Carb: 9g | Cholesterol: 17mg | Sodium: 431mg | Fat: 9g | Fiber: 4g

12. KETO SLOW COOKER PEPPER JACK CAULIFLOWER SIDE DISH

Preparation: 10 minutes | **Cooking:** 4 hours | **Serve:** 6

INGREDIENTS:

- Cauliflower heads, cut florets – 1 Head
- Whipped cream - ¼ Cup
- Cream cheese – 4 Ounces
- Pepper Jack, shredded – 4 Ounces
- Bacon cooked and crumbled – 6 slices
- Butter – 2 Tablespoon
- Pepper, grounded - ½ Teaspoon
- Sal to taste

INSTRUCTIONS:

1. Grease a 4-quart crockpot slow cooker slightly.
2. Put cauliflower, whipped cream, cream cheese, pepper, salt, and butter into the crockpot.
3. Set to slow cook for 3 hours.
4. After 3 hours, add pepper jack and stir properly to combine.
5. Continue cooking for about one hour, until the cauliflower becomes tender.
6. Add crumbled bacon on it.
7. Serve hot.

Cooking tip: You can add other fresh vegetables to increase the vegetable contents.

NUTRITIONAL VALUES

Cal: 272 | Carb: 6.1g | Fat: 21.29g | Protein: 10.79g | Fiber: 2.01g

KETO CROCK POT SWEETS

1. CROCK POT SUGAR FREE CHOCOLATE MOLTEN LAVA CAKE

Preparation time: 10 minutes | **Cooking time**: 3 hours | **Servings:** 12

INGREDIENTS

- Swerve sweetener divided - 1½ cup
- Gluten free flour - ½ cup
- Unsweetened cocoa powder divided - 5 tablespoons
- Sugar free chocolate chips - 4 ounces
- Baking powder - 1 teaspoon
- Butter melted, cooled - ½ cup
- Whole eggs - 3
- Egg yolks - 3
- Vanilla extract - 1 teaspoon

- Vanilla liquid stevia - ½ teaspoon
- Hot water - 2 cups
- Salt - ½ teaspoon

METHOD

1. Start with lubricating your crock pot.
2. Secondly mix 1¼ cup Swerve, flour, 3 tablespoons cocoa powder, salt and baking powder in a large bowl.
3. Then mix melted butter, after cooling with eggs, liquid stevia, vanilla extract, and yolks, in another small bowl.
4. Now mix both ingredients.
5. After mixing properly pour them into a crock pot.
6. Make the top with Choco chips.
7. Then in a small bowl blend the balance swerve sweetener and cocoa powder in hot water.
8. After mixing pour it on the Choco chops layer.
9. Then cook it on gas till 3 hours.
10. After cooking allow it to cool slightly.

Cooking tips: You can avoid the possibility of edge burning, which is a common problem you may face, by using parchment paper. Line your slow cooker with parchment paper.

NUTRITIONAL VALUES: Calories: 157 | Calories from Fat: 117 | Fat: 20% | Cholesterol: 39% | Sodium: 7% | Carbohydrates: 4% | Protein: 8%

2. LEMON CROCK POT CAKE

Preparation time: 10 minutes | **Cooking time:** 3 hours | **Servings:** 8

INGREDIENTS:

For cake

- Yellow cornmeal - ½ cup
- Sour cream - 1 cup
- All-purpose flour 1¾ cup
- Baking powder - 1 teaspoon
- Baking soda – 1 teaspoon
- Sugar - 1¼ cups
- Butter melted - ¾ cup
- Lemon zest grated – 1 tablespoon
- Vanilla extract – 1 teaspoon
- Poppy seeds - 1½ teaspoons
- Eggs – 2
- Salt - ½ teaspoon

Glaze

- Sugar – 1 cup
- Lemon juice - 2½ tablespoons

METHOD

1. Grease a 6-quart slow cooker and line it with parchment paper. Make sure to keep the parchment paper to cover till the up side of the cooker.
2. Mix cornmeal, flour, baking soda, baking powder, and salt in a medium bowl. Keep it aside.
3. Beat sugar and butter by using an electric mixer until it becomes smooth. 2-3 minutes beating would be fine.
4. Add eggs and continue beating for another 2 minutes.
5. Run the mixer on low speed and add lemon zest, sour cream, poppy seeds and vanilla extract.
6. Gradually add flour mixture to the jar and continue mixing.
7. Transfer the batter over the parchment liner to the cooker.
8. Cover the cooker and set cooking at a high temperature about 2½ hours.
9. Turn off the crock pot and remove the lid. Check the center with a knife or toothpick, whether it comes out smoothly.
10. Take a small bowl and whisk sugar and lemon juice.
11. Remove the cake from the crock pot and transfer to the wire rack and let it cool.

12. Sprinkle the glaze mix on top of the cake.

Serving tips: It may sound very delicious if served cold.

Cooking tip: Use parchment paper while baking cakes and place it up to the edge of the baking tray to avoid edge over burning issues, which is a common problem you may face while baking cakes.

NUTRITIONAL VALUES

Calories: 339 | Total Fat: 50% | Sodium: 9% | Carbohydrates: 4% | Dietary Fiber: 20% | Protein: 15%

3. KETO SLOW COOKER PUMPKIN CUSTARD

Preparation time: 10 minutes | **Cooking time:** 2 hours 45 minutes | **Servings:** 6

INGREDIENTS

- Pumpkin puree - 1 cup
- Eggs - 4
- Erythritol blend or Stevia granulated - ½ cup
- Vanilla extract - 1 teaspoon
- Almond flour - ½ cup
- Pumpkin spice - 1 teaspoon
- Ghee/butter - 4 tablespoons
- Salt to taste

METHOD

1. Grease a 4-quart slow cooker with butter or ghee.
2. Take a bowl and beat the eggs using a mixer.
3. Add sweetener and continue beating.
4. Now put vanilla and pumpkin puree to the beaten egg and continue blending.
5. Put pumpkin spice, almond flour, and salt. Blend again.
6. Add ghee/butter and continue blending.
7. Now transfer all the mixture to the slow cooker.
8. Keep a paper towel over the crock pot and close the lid.
9. The paper towel can absorb the moisture so that moisture will not drop back to the custard.
10. Start the slow cooker for about 2.45 hours.
11. After crossing 2 hours, check it frequently.
12. Once you find the side of the custard starts to pull away from the crock side and the center become firm, you can switch off the crock pot in another few minutes.
13. Top it with stevia whipped cream or spreading nutmeg or nuts as you like.
14. Serve warm or refrigerated

Baking tips: You can change the flavor as per your taste by keeping one batch for a flavor and another batch for a different flavor. For making more like a cake texture, you can add ¼ cup almond flour extra.

NUTRITIONAL VALUES: Calories: 147 | Total Fat: 12g | Cholesterol: 12mg | Carbohydrates: 4g | Dietary Fiber: 1g | Protein: 5g

4. KETO SUGAR & DAIRY FREE FUDGE

Preparation time: 5 minutes | **Cooking time:** 2 hours | **Serving:** 30

INGREDIENTS

- Sugarless chocolate chips - 2½ cups
- Vanilla extract - 1 teaspoon
- Coconut milk - ⅓ cups
- Vanilla stevia, liquid - 2 teaspoons
- Salt to taste

METHOD

1. In a 4-quart crock pot put vanilla, coconut milk, stevia, chocolate chips and stir well.
2. Add salt to taste.
3. Cover the cooker and slot heat about 2 hours.
4. Switch off the stove and let it cool for about 1 hour.
5. Open and stir it to smooth.
6. Now take a 1-quart casserole dish and line with parchment paper.
7. Spread the mix.
8. Refrigerate it for about 30 minutes or until it becomes firm.
9. Serve chilled.

Making tip: Vanilla stevia is optional. You can try different flavor to have different taste of your choice.

NUTRITIONAL VALUES

Calories: 65 | Total Fat: 5g | Carbohydrates: 2g | Dietary Fiber: 1.22g | Protein: 1g

5. CROCKPOT LEMON CAKE

Preparation time: 10 minutes | **Cooking time:** 3 hours | **Servings:** 8

INGREDIENTS

- Coconut flour - ½ Cup
- Almond flour - ½ Cup
- Pyure all purpose – 3 Tablespoons
- Baking powder – 2 Teaspoons
- Butter melted - ½ Cup
- Whipping cream - ½ Cup
- Lemon Juice – 2 Tablespoon
- Zest from two lemons
- Eggs – 2 Nos.
- Xanthan gum (Optional) - ½ Teaspoon

For Topping:

- Pyure all purpose – 3 Tablespoons
- Butter, melted – 2 Tablespoons
- Lemon juice – 2 Tablespoons
- Water, hot (boiled) - ½ Cup

INSTRUCTIONS:

1. In a bowl mix coconut flour, almond flour, sweetener, xanthan gum, and baking powder.
2. In another bowl whisk whipping cream, butter, zest, lemon juice, and egg.
3. Now add the dry mix to the wet mix and mix well until it becomes smooth.
4. Transfer the mix to a 4-quart crockpot cooker.
5. Line the crockpot with aluminum foil before transferring the mixture.
6. Now you need to do the topping.
7. Mix the topping ingredients in a bowl and pour on top of batter in the crockpot.
8. Start low cooking for about 3 hours.
9. Check after three hours by inserting a toothpick and if it comes off clean. Make sure, the batter is not sticking on the toothpick.
10. Serve medium hot.
11. Serve with whipped cream and fresh fruit.

Tips: Instead of Pyure, you can use Serve. If you want to serve the cake cold, keep the cake in the fridge for about 6-8 hours.

NUTRITIONAL VALUE

Cal: 350 | Carb: 9g | Fat: 32.6g | Sodium: 224mg | Protein: 7.6g | Dietary Fiber: 4.9g

6. SLOW COOKER PUMPKIN CUSTARD DESSERT

Preparation time: 10 minutes | **Cooking time:** 2 Hours and 40 Minutes | **Servings:** 6

INGREDIENTS:

- Pumpkin puree
- Stevia granulated or Erythritol blend
- Eggs, large – 4 Nos.
- Almond flour, superfine grade - ½ Cups
- Pumpkin pie spice – 1 Teaspoon
- Butter – 4 Tablespoons
- Ghee – 4 Tablespoons
- Vanilla extract – 1 Teaspoon
- Salt to taste
- Nutmeg for topping

INSTRUCTIONS:

1. In a 4-quart crockpot, grease the bottom by using butter or coconut spray.
2. Whisk the eggs in a bowl. Blend it by using an electric mixer and continue blending until it forms thick.
3. Add sweetener gradually while it is blending.
4. Now add vanilla and pumpkin puree and blend it slowly.
5. Add almond flour, pumpkin pie spice, and salt and continue blending.
6. While blending continues, add butter and ghee.
7. After blending it thoroughly, transfer the batter to crockpot.
8. Keep an aluminum liner before you transfer the batter to the crockpot.
9. Keep a paper towel by covering over the crockpot and cover the crockpot lid.
10. The paper towel is using to absorb the moisture to avoid spoiling the custard.
11. Set the cooker for 2 hours and 45 minutes.
12. Start checking the custard after 2 hours.
13. If you can see the custard start to pull away from the side of the crockpot, then the custard is getting ready.
14. Once done, serve warm with stevia whipped cream.
15. Sprinkle nutmeg before serving.

Tips: For pumpkin puree, you can also use canned one available in the stores. Instead of ghee, you can alternatively use virgin coconut oil. Vanilla is an essence to give flavor, and if you want to use any different flavor, you can use as per your preference.

NUTRITIONAL VALUE

Cal: 147 | Carb: 4g | Fat: 12g | Protein: 5g | Fiber: 1g

7. CROCKPOT SUGAR-FREE CHOCOLATE MOLTEN CAKE

Preparation time: 10 minutes | **Cooking time:** 3 hours | **Servings:** 12

INGREDIENTS:

- Unsweetened cocoa powder – 5 Tablespoons
- Gluten-free flour - ½ Cup
- Swerve sweetener - 1½ Cup
- Baking powder – 1 Teaspoon
- Butter melted - ½ Cup
- Egg – 3 Nos.
- Egg yolk – 3 Nos.
- Vanilla extract – 1 Teaspoon
- Sugar-free chocolate chips – 4 Ounces
- Vanilla liquid stevia - ½ Teaspoon

- Hot water – 2 cups
- Salt - ½ Teaspoon

INSTRUCTIONS:

1. Slightly grease the crockpot.
2. Whisk 1¼ cup of Swerve, 3 tablespoons cocoa powder, flour, baking powder and salt together in a bowl.
3. Take another medium bowl and mix eggs yolk, eggs, melted butter, liquid stevia and vanilla extract.
4. Mix the dry ingredients to the wet ingredient and blend it properly.
5. Transfer the batter to the crockpot.
6. Keep an aluminum liner in the pot before your transfer the batter.
7. Sprinkle chocolate chips on the top.
8. Now in another bowl mix the remaining cocoa powder, balance swerve sweetener in hot water.
9. Pour the mix over the top of the chocolate chips.
10. Place a paper towel over the crockpot and cover with the pot lid.
11. Set the cooker for low 3 hours.
12. Check the cake, after two hours by inserting a toothpick.
13. Serve after cooling.

Tips: Vanilla extract is using to maintain the flavor of the cake. You can choose any extract other than vanilla as per your preference.

NUTRITIONAL VALUE

Cal: 157 | Carb: 9.5g | Cholesterol: 117mg | Sodium: 166mg | Protein: 3.9g | Dietary Fiber: 2.6g

8. CARROT CAKE WITH CREAM CHEESE

Preparation time: 15 minutes | **Cooking time**: 4 hours | **Servings:** 12

INGREDIENTS

- Almond flour – 1½ Cups
- Swerve sweetener - ¾ Cups
- Coconut shredded - ½ Cup
- Eggs – 4 Nos.
- Walnuts, chopped - ½ Cup
- Whey protein powder, unflavored - ¼ Cup
- Baking powder – 2 Teaspoons
- Cinnamon, grounded – 1 Teaspoon
- Carrots, grated – 2 Cups
- Cloves, grounded - ¼ Teaspoon
- Coconut oil, virgin - ¼ Cup
- Almond milk – 3 Tablespoon
- Vanilla extract ½ Teaspoon
- Salt - ¼ Teaspoon

For Cream Cheese Frosting:

- Cream cheese, soft – 6 Ounces
- Vanilla extract - ¾ Teaspoon
- Swerve Sweetener, powder - ½ Cup
- Heavy cream - ½ Cup

DIRECTIONS:

1. Grease the slow crockpot.
2. Line the pot on the inside walls and bottom by using a quality parchment paper.
3. Whisk sweetener, almond flour, shredded coconut, protein powder, chopped nuts, baking powder, clove and cinnamon in a bowl.
4. Add salt.
5. In another bowl, whisk coconut oil, eggs, shredded carrots, vanilla extract, and almond milk and combine properly.
6. Mix both ingredients and transfer the batter to the crockpot.
7. Cover a paper towel on top of the crockpot and cover the lid.
8. Set the slow crockpot on cook for three and half hours.
9. Check after three hours and by inserting a toothpick to come off freely.
10. Once cooked, by holding parchment edges, lift out the cake gently.
11. Serve on a platter.

Tips: You can use pecans, instead of walnuts.

NUTRITIONAL VALUE

Cal: 245 | Carb: 9.5g | Fiber: 4.14g | Cholesterol: 92mg | Protein: 9.36g | Sodium: 229mg

9. CROCK POT BLUEBERRY LEMON CUSTARD CAKE

Preparation time: 15 minutes | **Cooking time:** 5.30 Hours | **Servings:** 12

INGREDIENTS

- Blueberries, fresh - ½ Cup
- Coconut flour - ½ Cup
- Eggs, separated – 6 Nos.
- Lemon juice - ⅓ Cup
- Lemon zest – 2 Teaspoon
- Liquid stevia – 1 Teaspoon
- Swerve sweetener - ½ Cup
- Light cream – 2 Cups
- Salt - ½ Teaspoon

DIRECTIONS:

1. Put the egg whites in a medium bowl and whip it with an electric mixer, until it becomes stiff and forming peaks. After that keep it aside.
2. Now beat the remaining yellow yolks, adding the remaining ingredients, excluding blueberries, in a medium bowl by using the electric mixer.
3. Add a small portion of the beaten egg white to the batter and mix gently and combine thoroughly.
4. Now clean your crockpot and transfer the batter to the pot.
5. Sprinkle the blueberries evenly on top of batter.
6. Cover the crockpot with a paper towel over the pot before covering the pot lid, so that the paper can prevent the moisture dropping back to the dessert.
7. Set to heat for about 3 hours.
8. After cooking done, remove the lid and paper cover and let it cool for some time.
9. Then refrigerate for 2 hours.
10. Serve cold.

Tips: Use sugar-free whipped cream, for people who are conscious about sugar intake. Instead of lemon zest and lemon juice, you can use alternative natural flavors of your choice for a change.

NUTRITIONAL VALUE

Cal: 140 | Carb: 7.3g | Fat: 9.2g | Protein: 3.9g | Cholesterol: 116mg | Dietary Fiber: 2.2g | Sodium: 167mg

10. LOW CARB CROCK POT MAPLE CUSTARD

Preparation time: 10 minutes | **Cooking time:** 3 hours | **Servings:** 6

INGREDIENTS:

- Eggs – 2 Nos.
- Egg yolks – 2
- Heavy organic cream – 1 Cup
- Low-fat milk - ½ Cup
- Sugar-free brown sweetener - ¼ Cup
- Maple extract – 1 teaspoon
- Cinnamon - ½ Teaspoon
- Salt - ¼ Teaspoon

DIRECTIONS:

1. Whisk all ingredients in a medium bowl using an electric mixer. Mix until combine it properly.
2. Now take ramekins with 4 ounces capacity and fill the batter ¾.
3. Keep the ramekins in the crockpot.
4. Cover the crockpot with a paper towel and cover the pot lid.
5. The paper towel can absorb the excess moisture released during cooking.
6. Set the cooker for 3 hours.
7. Check occasionally to make sure the cooking position.
8. Take out the ramekins and let it cool and refrigerate to chill for about 2 hours.
9. Serve with sugar-free whipped cream.
10. Sprinkle cinnamon powder on top.

Tips: You can change the maple extract to vanilla or cherry or anything as per your preference. So, when you change the flavor, the custard also will change its identity.

NUTRITIONAL VALUE

Cal: 190 | Carb: 2g | Fat: 18g | Cholesterol: 176mg | Protein: 4g | Sodium: 144mg | Potassium: 83mg

11. CROCK POT LEMON CUSTARD

Preparation time: 10 minutes | **Cooking time:** 3 hours | **Servings:** 4

INGREDIENTS:

- Lemon zest – 1 Tablespoon
- Lemon juice - ¼ Cup
- Egg yolks – 5 Nos.
- Liquid stevia - ½ Teaspoon
- Vanilla extract – 1 Teaspoon
- Whipped cream – 2 Cups
- Fresh mixed fruits, diced - ¼ Cups

DIRECTIONS:

1. Whisk vanilla, lemon zest, egg yolks, liquid stevia and lemon juice in a medium-size bowl.
2. Add the heavy cream and continue whisking until combine thoroughly.
3. Now take ramekins and transfer the batter to each slot.
4. After that place the cooking rack in the crockpot and place the ramekins on top.
5. Pour water in the crockpot to cover the ramekins until half of its side level.
6. Set the crockpot for 3 hours and start cooking.
7. Before covering lid, cover the crockpot with a paper towel so that towel can absorb the moisture released during cooking.
8. Check it after 3 hours and remove it from the cooker and let it cool.
9. Refrigerate it for another 3 hours before serve.
10. Serve with whipped cream, sprinkled with mix fruits.

Tips: Instead of whipped cream, you can use slightly sweetened coconut whipped cream. You can also change the sweetener to any of your choices.

NUTRITIONAL VALUE

Cal: 319 | Carb: 3g | Dietary Fiber: 0g | Protein: 7g | Fat: 41g

12. KETO MOCHA PUDDING CAKE

Preparation time: 8 minutes | **Cooking time:** 2 hours 30 minutes |
Other Time: 30 minutes | **Servings:** 6

INGREDIENTS

- Butter or coconut oil spray for greasing the slow cooker
- Unsweetened chocolate, chopped finely - 2 Ounces
- Butter, cut into large chunks - ¾ cup
- Instant coffee crystals - 2 tablespoons
- Heavy cream - ½ cup
- Almond flour- ⅓ cup
- Vanilla extract- 1 tablespoon
- Unsweetened cocoa powder - 4 tablespoons
- Large eggs - 5
- Stevia/erythritol granulated sweetener - ⅔ cup
- Salt - ⅛ tablespoon
- Optional: whipped cream or ice cream (both low carb) for serving.

METHOD

1. Grease your slow crock pot cooker, preferably a 6-quart size with butter/coconut oil.
2. On low heat, melt unsweetened chocolate and butter in a saucepan and whisk completely.
3. Remove it from heat and allow it to settle.
4. Now mix coffee crystals, heavy cream, vanilla extract and coffee crystals in a small bowl.
5. Mix cocoa, salt and almond flour, in a medium bowl.
6. Beat eggs in a large bowl with an electric mixer on high speed until slightly thickened.
7. Add sweetener gradually.
8. Beat on high speed until it becomes thick and pale yellow for about 5 minutes.
9. Turn down the mixer speed and mix the unsweetened chocolate and melted butter mixture slowly.

10. Stir in salt, almond flour and cocoa mixture.
11. Keeping the mixer at medium speed, add the cream, vanilla, coffee, and mix gradually, and then pour the batter into slow cooker.
12. For absorbing condensation, keep a paper towel over the opening of the slow cooker before you place the lid.
13. Cook on low for 2-3 hours or 2.5 to 3.5 hours if you are using a 6 quart or a 4-quart slow cooker respectively.
14. When you are about to finish the baking, the center will be bit softer than the edges. The center top will be slightly damp but slightly bounce back when you press gently. The temperature at the center should reach 70 degrees Celsius for a perfect backing.
15. Top it with whipped cream or even garnishing with low carb ice cream.

Cooking tips: Place a paper towel over the opening of the slow cooker, before you shut the cooker's lid. In doing so it can absorb condensation. Condensation will spoil the cooking.

NUTRITIONAL VALUES

Calories: 413.5 | Fats: 39.81g | Net Carbs: 3.76g | Protein: 9.29g

SHOPPING LIST

The following are the list of ingredients most commonly used for preparing these recipes.

All these listed items are readily available in the super markets and can store at home for a long period, because of the extended shelve life. These recipes are quick to cook, tailored to meet the expectation of people who have a busy professional life.

Fruits	Apple
	Avocado
	Banana
	Green apple
	Blueberries
Vegetables	Pumpkin
	Tomato
	Onion
	Red onion
	Cauliflower
	Brown Jicama
	Radish
	Bacon
	Carrot
	Yellow onion
	Green bell pepper
	Mushroom
	Button mushroom
	Spinach
	Coriander leaves
	Cilantro leaves
	Celery
	Sweet potato
	Yam
	Napa cabbage
	Basil
	Green pepper
	Zucchini
	Parsley
	Chives
	Thyme

	Baby spinach
	Mozzarella
	Fresh tapioca
	Poblano pepper
	Fresh garlic
	Scallions
	Pesto green
	Pesto red
	Red pepper
	Celery
	Jalapeno chili pepper
	Eggplant
	Yellow summer squash
	Bay leaves
	Kale
	Red pepper (Sweet)
	Garlic
	Marjoram
	Rosemary
	Zest of orange
	Sage
	Rutabaga
	Cabbage leaves
	Asparagus stalks
	Dill
	White mushrooms
	Italian herbs
	Ginger
	Sprouts
Non-Veg items	Chicken
	Chicken wings
	Chicken breast
	Chicken wing drummettes
	Boneless skinless chicken thigh
	Frozen meatballs
	Beef
	Beef lean
	Pork ribs
	Pork sausage
	Eggs
	Breakfast sausage
	Cooked ham

	Smoked deli ham
	Turkey sausage
	Turkey thighs
	Crab meat
	Boneless lamb
	Italian sausage
	Caned light tuna
Grains	Black beans
	Rice
	Artichoke hearts
	White beans
	Dry mustard
	Dijon mustard
	Black beans
	White kidney beans
	Dill
	Coriander seeds
	Cumin seeds
	Dried oregano
	Dry vermouth
	Yellow mustard seeds
	Pomegranate seeds
	Poppy seeds
Liquids	Milk
	Low fat milk
	Vinegar
	Balsamic vinegar
	Greek yogurt
	Apricot syrup
	Maple syrup
	Bourbon
	Water
	Lemon juice
	Lime juice
	Salt free tomato paste
	Vegetable broth
	Chicken broth
	Rice wine vinegar
	Balsamic vinegar
	Beef stock
	Orange juice
	Red wine

	Vanilla extract
	Vanilla liquid stevia
	Celery soup
	Tamari Soy
	Pyure
	Almond milk sweetened
Puree	Pumpkin puree
Oil/Cheese	Olive oil
	Coconut oil
	Sesame oil
	Avocado oil
	Pepper Jack cheese
	Cheddar cheese
	Feta cheese
	Butter
	Cottage cheese
	Gorgonzola
	Neufchatel cheese
	Parmesan cheese
	Mozzarella
	Blue cheese
	Ghee
	Gruyere cheese
	Coconut butter
Creams	Sour cream
	Heavy white cream
	Cream cheese
	Heavy organic cream
	Mayo
	Sour cream
	Low carb whipped cream
	Grape jelly
	Blue cheese
	Low carb ice cream
Sauce	Salsa
	Hot sauce
	Soy sauce
	Plum sauce
	Hoisin sauce
	Buffalo wing sauce
	Tomato sauce
	Tomato paste

	Peanut sauce
	Marinara sauce
	Ketchup
	Worcestershire sauce
	Chili sauce
	Tamari Soy sauce
	Chimichurri sauce
Spices	Garlic powder
	Mustard powder
	Coriander powder
	Cumin powder
	Chili powder
	Pepper powder
	Onion powder
	Psyllum husk powder
	Clove
	Five spice powder
	Cayenne pepper powder
	Ginger grounded
	Smoked paprika
	Dried oregano
	Chipotle powder
	Turmeric powder
	Spanish Paprika
	Pumpkin spice
	Cocoa powder
	Vanilla bean powder
	Xanthan gum
	Cinnamon powder
Flavor to taste	Salt
	Kosher salt
	Baking powder
	Sea salt
	Erythritol
	Vanilla liquid stevia
	Lemon zest
	Coconut aminos
	Keto MCT Oil powder
Sweetener	Swerve
	Sugar
	Low carb sweetener
	Sugar free brown sweetener

	Granulated sweetener
Flour	Gluten free flour
	Almond flour
	Whey protein powder
	Unsweetened cocoa powder
	Coconut flour
	Almond flour
	Stevia powder
	All-purpose flour
	Yellow cornmeal
Nuts	Hazel nuts
	Almonds
	Water chestnuts
	Nutmeg
	Almond meal
	Walnuts
	Flaxseed meal
Misc.	Potato dippers
	Breadcrumbs
	Protein bits
	Pita chips
	Tortilla chips
	Pitted olives
	Multigrain baguette slices
	Wheat pita chips
	Tapioca flour
	Cocoa powder
	Baking powder
	Chocolate chips
	Baking soda
	Sugar free dark chocolate
	Crackers
	Sugar free Nutella spread
	Sugar free chocolate chips
	Sweetened chocolate chips
	Instant coffee crystals

EQUIPMENT AND TOOLS USED IN THE RECIPES

List of most commonly used utensils, kitchenware and cutleries

Keto Crockpot 4-Quart
Keto Crockpot 6-Quart
Slow cooker 4-Quart
Slow cooker 6-Quart
Food processor
Electric mixer
Sausage pan
Mixing bowl
Knife
Wooden spatula
Wooden spoon
Skillet
Tablespoon
Teaspoon
Paper Towel
Aluminum Foil

CONCLUSION

This book is deeply committed to serving you with love, refinement, and compassion so that you may reach your weight loss goals quickly with these easy Keto recipes. I believe in the healing power of healthy and nourishing food. I look forward to democratizing health care by nurturing self-responsibility for healing and restoring your body with nutrition and love. I'm grateful to be a part of your health and weight loss journey.

Thank you for purchasing this book. I sincerely hope that this Keto diet plan will be your biggest inspiration to eat healthy all the time. I have included diet plans that are convenient and suitable for everyone. I wish you a happy dieting and live your healthy life to the fullest!

Thank you

Made in the USA
Monee, IL
08 January 2020